CONTRASTIVE RHETORIC REVISITED AND REDEFINED

CONTRASTIVE RHETORIC REVISITED AND REDEFINED

Edited by

Clayann Gilliam Panetta
Christian Brothers University

LEA LAWRENCE ERLBAUM ASSOCIATES, PUBLISHERS
2001   Mahwah, New Jersey   London

Lawrence Erlbaum Associates, Inc., Publishers
10 Industrial Avenue
Mahwah, NJ 07430

Cover design by Kathryn Houghtaling Lacey

Library of Congress Cataloging-in-Publication Data

Contrastive rhetoric revisited and redefined / edited by Clayann Gilliam
Panetta
    p. cm.
  Includes bibliographical references and index.
  ISBN 0-8058-3634-9 (cloth : alk. paper) — ISBN 0-8058-3635-7 (pbk. :
  alk. paper)
  Rhetoric—Study and teaching. 2. Contrastive linguistics. 3. English
  language—Study and teaching—Foreign speakers. I. Panetta, Clayann
  Gilliam
  P53.27.C67   2000   00-034085
                                                              CIP

Books published by Lawrence Erlbaum Associates are printed on acid-free
paper, and their bindings are chosen for strength and durability.

Printed in the United States of America
10 9 8 7 6 5 4 3 2 1

Contents

Foreword
What in the World Is
Contrastive Rhetoric?

Robert B. Kaplan
Professor Emeritus
University of Southern California

Contrastive rhetoric (CR),[1] although it has been available in the United States for about 35 years (Kaplan, 1966), has had virtually no impact on the traditional composition classroom in the United States (but see Villanueva, 1995). The reasons are fairly clear: Traditional composition teachers have tended to assume that they are addressing a monolingual, monocultural population (Kaplan, in press-c). Contrary to that assumption, students who are not native speakers of Standard American Schooled English (SASE) and who do not participate to any significant degree in the dominant U.S. cultural traditions have been entering composition classrooms in ever-increasing numbers through most of the last half of the 20th century.[2] They are likely to continue to do so, despite the fulminations of various conservative legislators who seek to have English declared the official language of the several states and of the United States and who seek to impose various draconian constraints on immigration.

---

[1]I have never been happy with the designation *theory* for the notion of contrastive rhetoric; by definition, a theory can be tested, but I fear the notion *contrastive rhetoric* cannot really be tested in a satisfactory manner, because any test will be contaminated by the emic/etic problem.

[2]Students who are not native speakers of SASE include (at least) foreign students, immigrants (legal and illegal), Native-American students, Black students, Hispanic students, a variety of other hyphenated-American students (e.g., Asian-American), permanent resident aliens, students with political asylum status, and a variety of students who do not subscribe to dominant cultural assumptions (e.g., gay and lesbian students). Within this group are individuals who have English as their only language, but whose English is not SASE.

Admittedly, CR came into existence with the intent of addressing the needs of individuals for whom English was not a first language—specifically, foreign students in U.S. tertiary institutions. Composition teachers have assumed that CR was exclusively for English-as-a-foreign-language (EFL) teaching and thus have felt justified in ignoring it. In the 1960s, the audio-lingual method was pretty well entrenched in ESL classrooms (and EFL classrooms too, for that matter). CR was intended to move learners beyond the memorization of dialogues, beyond regurgitation of set patterns, beyond exclusive concern with grammatical accuracy, and beyond concern only with the sentence. It was intended to facilitate reading and writing in English, creative use of the second language, and the ability to express one's ideas in text in the second language. Thus, it was not initially directed at the teacher in conventional (presumably) monolingual, monocultural environments. Since the 1960s, however, its usefulness in other environments has been discussed (Connor, 1996; Panetta, chap. 1, this volume).

CR assumes that languages differ not only in phonological, morphological, and grammatical features, but in the kinds of genres available to their speakers for the organization of discourse and in the rhetorical (and syntactic) features that co-occur with those genres.[3] This is not to suggest that the differences in syntactic and phonological features between English and a number of other languages have been ignored; on the contrary, a substantial number (see, e.g., Moulton, 1963; Stockwell & Bowen, 1965; Stockwell & Martin, 1965) of "contrastive analyses" of syntactic features are available in the literature, as are a number of studies of CR between English and other languages.[4] These con-

---

[3]The term *contrastive* was adopted in the mid-1960s to differentiate "contrastive rhetoric" from the rash of "comparative" syntactic studies being undertaken at the time, the latter largely based on an early version of error analyses. It is implicit in the term *contrastive* that the rhetorics meeting across cultures and languages were also necessarily competitive (see, e.g., the discussion in Corbett, chap. 3, this volume).

[4]Specifically, Arabic (Hatim, 1991; Ostler, 1987; Sa'Adeddin, 1987, 1989); Australian Aboriginal languages/English (Eggington, 1990); "Chicano" Spanish/English (Montaño-Harmon, 1988, 1991); Chichewa (Chimombo, 1988); Chinese (Standard Written Chinese; Bloch, 1989; Campbell, 1989; Cheng, 1985; Dunkleblau, 1990; Scollon, 1991; Tsao, 1983); Finnish (Mauranen, 1993); French, Georgian, German (Clyne, 1987; Skyum-Nielsen & Schröder, 1994); Hebrew (Folman & Connor, 1992; Folman & Sarig, 1990); Hindi (Kachru, 1983); Japanese (Hinds, 1987, 1990; Neustupny, 1997); Korean (Chang, 1983); Marathi (Pandharipanda, 1983); Native-American Languages/English (Leap, 1983); Portuguese (Dantas-Whitney & Grabe, 1992); Romanian (Manoliu-Manea, 1995); Russian, Spanish (Mexican, Puerto Rican, etc.; Kamhi-Stein, 1995; Lux, 1991; Lux & Grabe, 1991; Ostler, 1992; Reid, 1988; Reppen & Grabe, 1993); Thai (Bickner & Peyasantiwong, 1988; Indrasutra, 1988); Turkish (Enginarlar, 1990; Oktar, 1991); Urdu (Baumgardner, 1987, 1992); Vietnamese (Soter, 1988). There is some work involving several languages; for example, English, French, and Arabic (Daoud, 1991; Reid, 1988); Dutch and other languages (Ulijn & Strother, 1995; Wijst & Ulijn, 1995); some of this work in particular registers/genres (e.g., business text in English and Japanese: Connor, 1989; Oi & Sato, 1990; conference abstracts in Chinese: Cantor, 1994); and there is some work on particular grammatical categories, for example, epistemic modals in Chicano English (Youmans,

trastive analyses (e.g., Kaplan et al., 1983), however, are largely restricted to the level of the sentence.[5] It is an assumption of CR that discourse is not simply a collection of (more or less) correct syntactic structures, but rather represents a complex multifaceted, multidimensional set (Connor, 1996; Scollon, 1997). Language is not—cannot be—an isolated system, and grammar cannot be equated with language. As Enkvist (1997) put it:

> The important point is to realize that the text is the father of the sentence, and that text strategies come before the syntactic formation of individual sentences. Giving a sentence its textual fit, its conformity with the text strategy, is not a cosmetic surface operation polishing the sentence after it is already there. Textual fit is a far more basic requirement, determining the choice of words as well as the syntactic structure of a sentence. To modern text and discourse linguists this is so obvious that it seems curious that grammarians and teachers of composition have, through the centuries, spent so much time and effort on syntactic phenomena within individual sentences, while overlooking the fundamental questions of text strategy and information flow. (p. 199)

A SET OF QUESTIONS

The individual who does not participate in the monolingual, monocultural assumptions that dominate the composition classroom is faced with five terrible questions:

1. What may be discussed?
2. Who has the authority to speak/write? Or: Who has the authority to write to whom under what circumstances?
3. What form(s) may the writing take?
4. What is evidence?
5. What arrangement of evidence is likely to appeal (be convincing) to readers?

1995). Some work has been directed specifically to ESL teaching (Ferris, 1991, 1992, 1993, 1994a, 1994b; Ferris & Hedgcock, 1998) or to language assessment (Weasenforth, 1995). Additionally an "eclectic philosophy of language" based on CR and rhetorical theory has been developed (Kowal, 1994). Biber (1988, 1992, 1995) introduced a multidimensional model of analysis employing complex computer-based techniques, and that model has been employed by some of the researchers enumerated here. Shirley Ostler at Bowling Green University has a number of the unpublished studies and is usually happy to share them for the cost of copying and postage; contact her at sostler@bgnet.bgsu.edu.

[5]In the 1970s and into the 1980s, empirical research was the dominant form; empirical research often involved counting various features in text. In that time frame, the features available for counting were syntactic features. Many of the early studies in CR were based on contrasts of the occurrence of countable features.

1. What May Be Discussed?   This question must occur to composition teachers when they assign essay topics. English speakers, for example, are loathe to discuss bathroom functions, whereas speakers of Thai have no problem with that topic. Because abortion is a political issue in the United States, it might be considered appropriate to assign, as a topic for a class essay, some discussion of issues surrounding abortion; after all, virtually every U.S. politician and virtually every newspaper and television editorial writer has a position on the matter. In Northern Europe (Finland, Norway, Sweden, etc.), abortion is exclusively a medical question, and the subject simply wouldn't be discussed. To illustrate, as Dellinger (in press) noted, for example:

> Abortion in Finland is a very personal issue, as are many such issues, including religion itself. If it [abortion] is discussed at all, then it is considered a medical question. In any case, because of the assumption that it has to do with medicine, it is not a political issue, and certainly does not belong to the public world of television news discourse.

On the other hand, in devoutly Roman Catholic countries (e.g., most of Latin America), the question is essentially taboo, as it is a religious issue not open to debate. It should not be surprising that speakers of other languages may seem to suffer from writer's block when such a topic is assigned.

2. Who Has the Authority to Speak/Write?   In U.S. composition tradition, anyone—even a lowly student—has the authority to write and to hold and express an opinion, but in more traditional cultures, the young have no such authority. As a consequence, students tend to quote (or at least parrot) those whom they perceive to have authority. "Youngsters" do not have the authority to hold a new or original opinion. In U.S. composition classrooms, learners so inhibited may be accused of failing to exercise critical thinking, but they may not see themselves as authorized to undertake such an act. Scollon (1991) showed that social hierarchy is carefully structured in Chinese society, that an individual of lower status must wait for an individual of higher status to invite communication, and that an individual of higher status has an obligation to do so. In English, the rules are not quite so clear except in extreme cases—for example, in interactions between a military officer and an ordinary soldier, or in interactions between a school administrator and a student (Kaplan, 1997). In the final analysis, it is the "expert" who has the authority to write—even in English.

> Experts are people who, through their publications and research, have reached wide audiences, whose opinions and views serve as authority sources, who have produced some of the key touchstones of the [discourse] community: [Shirley Brice] Heath's and [Elinore] Ochs' work on language socialization, [R. B.] Kaplan's research in contrastive rhetoric, [William] Labov's analysis of narrative, [John] Swales' work on genres, [Deborah] Tannen's work in discourse analysis, among

others. All of these individuals ["experts"] have long-standing influence on the field [of Applied Linguistics]: Their work serves as templates on which the rest of the [discourse] community builds, and their thoughts are embodied in specific textual forms particular to academic writing. (Ramanathan & Kaplan, 2000)

Young students do not have such authority and may be reluctant to venture any opinion, or may be unable to discuss the topic because it does not occur in their first-language discourse.

3. What Form(s) May the Writing Take? This is really a question of available genres. It is an assumption of CR that genres are nothing more nor less than conventional solutions to recurring communication problems. Although students who are native speakers of other languages may bring with them a rich inventory of genres, there may be a mismatch between the genres in the other language and those in English, or the genres may serve unexpected purposes, or the co-occurring syntactic features may be quite different. Most speakers of English recognize that a sonnet, for example, is a poetic form and that it would probably be inappropriate to present a cooking recipe in the form of a sonnet, and most English-speaking readers would be likely to reject a sonnet which merely conveys a cooking recipe. The subject matter of sonnets is part of "what everybody knows." Berkenkotter and Huckin (1993) suggested that "knowledge production [in different disciplines] is carried out and codified largely through generic forms of writing: lab reports, working papers, reviews, grant proposals, technical reports, conference papers, journal articles, monographs and so forth" (p. 476). The generic form plays an important role in the process of knowledge dissemination. "Kaplan's (1966) controversial 'doodles' article would not have fueled research in contrastive rhetoric had he written it in the form of a memo, for instance. For one thing, *Language Learning* would not have accepted it for publication" (Ramanathan & Kaplan, 2000).

The speaker of another language or variety brings with her or him a rich inventory of various genres; the problem is that those genres may be utterly inappropriate in an English-speaking academic context (see Woolever, chap. 4, this volume). The sets of genres in different languages may not overlap to any significant degree; it is a serious fallacy to assume that the genres of English are in some way universal. Trueba (1986) wrote:

Issues regarding "language handicaps" and "academic underachievement," are social phenomena that surface in the form of linguistic deviance and are then "interpreted by the experts." The traditional assessment of concept formation is based on the assumption that, if the child does not demonstrate in an appropriate linguistic form that s/he recognizes a concept (or concepts) and its (their) interrelationships in those domains "all normal children" know, the child is handicapped. A perfectly normal child who has just arrived from a linguistically, socially, and culturally different country [or community], by not being able to produce in oral or written text the expected linguistic forms, becomes—ipso facto—"abnormal" in the eyes of the educator. (p. 48)

4. What Is Evidence? The question of the nature of evidence is critical. First there is the problem of fact versus opinion. Learners of English as a second or foreign language often are misled by the use of such devices as the factive opener in English; a sentence that begins with the phrase "it is true that . . ." (or some similar structure) may indeed transmit an unsubstantiated opinion despite its opener. Furthermore, learners often cannot differentiate the relative weight in authority between something that appears in a weekly newsmagazine and something that appears in a scholarly journal. Students arriving from traditional cultures may be inclined to quote, as authority, the content of canonical religious texts or the writings of famous historical figures.

Some years ago, a student of mine—a Saudi Arabian and a devout Muslim—wrote a class paper for me, in a language policy course, on the rise and fall of world languages. When he treated Greek, Latin, French, and English, he was able to bring to bear economic, social, historical, political, military, and other pertinent factors, but when he discussed Arabic, he was only able to say that Arabic was the language of Allah and of the Holy Koran. His religious orthodoxy prevented him from exploring evidence pertaining to his own language. The only pertinent evidence he could invoke derived from the special status of that language.

5. What Arrangement of Evidence Is Likely to Appeal to Readers? This final question is really a question of audience. Novice writers may not be aware of audience considerations. No matter what teachers say about audience, novice writers understand intuitively that they are writing for the teacher, because it is the teacher who has authority over the text (i.e., the assignment of a grade; see Bliss, chap. 2, this volume). Novice writers coming from different linguistic systems may have different assumptions about the appropriate form of address to the teacher (or any audience).[6] All novice writers, but especially writers who are not native speakers of English, understand that a teacher is an authority figure, but:

• They may have difficulty perceiving any distinction between "the person who may be addressed" (in the system from which they come) and the teacher.

---

[6]It is important to remember that few other educational systems give as much attention to writing as the U.S. system does (see, e.g., Kaplan, 1995). It is also important to remember that assumptions about age, race, gender, and socioeconomic class (deriving from the student's background) will color the text produced.

- They may fail to understand that the teacher is (on the other hand) not exactly like a peer, whom the student knows how to address.
- They may underestimate the teacher's ability to identify stylistic differences and catch plagiarism.

Mauranen (1993), in a contrastive study of Finnish and English, showed that writers differ in their culturally determined rhetorical practices, and that these differences manifest themselves in typical discourse features and in the way the writers are perceived by readers:

> [Writers] differ in some of their culturally determined rhetorical practices, and these differences manifest themselves in typical textual features. *The writers seem not to be aware of these textual features, or the underlying rhetorical practices.* This lack of awareness is in part due to the fact that textlinguistic features have not been the concern of traditional language teaching in schools. Sometimes text strategies are taught for the mother tongue, but rarely if ever for foreign languages separately. Such phenomena have therefore not been brought to the attention of [writers] struggling with writing. . . . *Nevertheless, these sometimes subtle differences between writing cultures, often precisely because they are subtle and not commonly observable to the non-linguist, tend to put . . . [various] native language [writers] at a rhetorical disadvantage in the eyes of [other language] readers. . . . This disadvantage is more than a difference in cultural tastes, since it may not only strike readers as lack of rhetorical elegance, but as lack of coherent writing or even [coherent] thinking, which can seriously affect the credibility of non-native writers.* (pp. 1–2; italics added)

These five terrible questions can be summed up in one overwhelming question: "Who writes what to whom, how, when, where, and to what end?" The first part of the question—*who writes what to whom*—implicates the basic relationship between reader and writer as well as the issue of "what may be discussed." The question is also impacted significantly by the performative abilities of both the writer and the reader. *How* implicates the question of the kind of evidence to be invoked. *When* implicates the chronology of the event involved; this is not a question of verb tense but rather a question of the existence of co-text.[7] There are no cooking-recipe sonnets to my knowledge, but there are lots of sonnets, produced over a long historical time. *Where* implicates the language to be used, the register appropriate to the act in a particular setting, and the pre-text that exists as a template for the act. *To what end* raises the question of audience; that is, what sort of response/reaction does the writer intend to evoke/provoke? These matters can be interrelated in a model

---

[7]The matter of co-text is most easily demonstrated through the development of science and technology texts. Science is, by definition, cumulative, every innovation based on a thick body of preceding science writing. Thus, every science text is "formed" on the basis of previously existing science text, and such forms as the scientific article are defined by the co-existence of a great body of other science texts (see, e.g., Atkinson, 1999; Kaplan, in press-b).

of writing (see, e.g., Grabe & Kaplan, 1996, for a number of different models, and Kaplan, in press-a, for the most recent iteration of a model that has been evolving over the past decade).

Learning these things about writing cannot be left to the learner's intuition; rather, these things have to be taught explicitly—anew in every generation (see Panetta, chap. 1, this volume). Halliday (1978) wrote:

> What is learning to read and to write? Fundamentally, it is an extension of the functional potential of language. Those children who don't learn to read and write, by and large, are children to whom it doesn't make sense; to whom the functional extension that these media provide has not been made clear, or does not match up with their own expectations of what language is for. Hence, if the child has not been oriented toward the types of meaning which the teacher sees as those which are proper to the writing system, then the learning of reading and writing would be out of context, because fundamentally, as in the history of the human race, reading and writing are an extension of the function of language. This is what they must be for the child [and for the L2 learner] equally well. (p. 57)

What Halliday said about reading and writing for the child is true also for second/foreign language learning (as distinct from acquisition) among children and adults—especially learning to read and write—to achieve literacy; if it doesn't make sense to the learner, there is little or no motivation to learn.

WHAT ABOUT CONVENTIONS?

Many so-called writing classes, both for native speakers and for those for whom SASE is not an available discourse, are not really "writing" classes at all; rather, they are classes about the surface of writing. This is not to say that the conventions of writing can be ignored; they are no more transparent than is the structure of discourse. The use and size of margins,[8] the numbering of pages,[9] the indentation of paragraphs, the use of hyphens (both in conjoined phrases and at the ends of lines),[10] the uses of punctuation and spacing,[11] the learning of spelling[12] (and the use of dictionaries)—all these have to be learned because there is nothing self-evident about them and because conventional practices vary widely across literate cultures. But these are not factors in writing—rather,

---

[8]In writing systems in which linear movement is right-to-left or top-to-bottom, the conventions governing margins are rather different than they are in left-to-right English.

[9]That is, the problem of where to put such numbers on the page and how to indicate continuation; for example, U.S. text doesn't, but various other systems use the abbreviation PTO (or its equivalent) to indicate onward movement.

[10]In nonsyllabic languages, line-end hyphenation does not occur between syllables.

[11]In character-based languages, each character occurs in the middle of an imaginary box; so too does punctuation.

[12]Semitic languages do not present vowels in the orthography.

they constitute important prewriting skills. Learning to write a passive structure is a prewriting grammatical skill, but learning when, where, why, and how to use a passive structure is indeed a function of writing.

WHAT ABOUT L1 INFLUENCES?

Writers select and arrange textual material in terms of their "abilities to convey just those analyses . . . of event[s] that are most compatible with the linguistic means provided by their languages" (Berman & Slobin, 1994, p. 12; see also Kellerman, 1995). The rich inventory of syntactic and discourse elements learners bring with them from their first language and from their prior education will color their writing in the second language. CR—which started its life as a means to get beyond the limitations of the audio-lingual approach to language teaching—now constitutes a notion that pervades rhetoric and composition issues across the curriculum and provides the means for teachers and students to understand why writing—which may be conventionally and syntactically "correct"—remains out of focus to readers of SASE. CR applies to learning to write in any population not highly practiced in SASE, and the absence of familiarity with SASE approaches may be derived at least from differences in gender (see Micciche, chap. 6, this volume), in ethnicity, in race (see Comfort, chap. 7, this volume), in sexual orientation (see McBeth, chap. 8, this volume), and in educational and experiential background.

WHAT'S WRONG WITH CR?

CR has been criticized as a notion steeped in xenophobia and restrictive of the learner's freedom to experiment with deviant forms of discourse. This is simply not the case. CR came into existence as a notion designed to help learners manage the discourse structure of SASE. To the extent that the use of SASE is xenophobic and framing of a particular power structure, CR is guilty of the charge. CR emerged as a notion designed to inculcate a standard of schooled discourse. To the extent that it does so, it is guilty of limiting learners' freedom to use other discourse structures. Learners are free to pursue whatever experimentation they wish, once they have control of some basic standard. To the extent that such experimentation may result in texts that constitute mazes defying comprehension, it may be inappropriate to encourage experimentation (see Scoggins, chap. 5, this volume). (Of course, it is the case that lack of discourse fluency may mask simple stupidity, but that is a separate issue, beyond the capacity of CR to explain and beyond the scope of this discourse.) CR has implications for any population that, for whatever reason, brings deviant rhetorical practices to texts written in SASE for SASE-speaking readers. It is conceived as a means of understanding SASE rhetoric, creating SASE discourse, and thereby achieving communication with SASE-speaking audiences. It was never intended to be replacive; rather, it was always perceived as being additive—contributing to the resources available for discourse-building among bilingual populations, whether that bilingualism/bidialectalism implicates another language, another variety of English, or any variety based on English but different from it in "significant" ways (e.g., African-American vernacular English, Asian-American vernacular English, Hispanic-American vernacular English, Native-American vernacular English—although these are labels that tend to group together significantly different population segments and to suggest unfortunate stereotypes). Significant ways may include semantics, morphology, grammar, and rhetoric, and in some cases phonology.

A COMPENDIUM

The chapters in this volume examine the issues as they pertain to various populations—gay and lesbian individuals, speakers of various hyphenated-American vernacular Englishes, women—and the ways in which the notion of CR contributes to an understanding of genre, curriculum, special-purpose writing (e.g., business), and the various transmission media. In an ideal world, the volume might have been expanded to consider other populations, for example, the deaf (users of ASL), the blind (users of Braille), and—of course—speakers of any number of particular languages; and the volume might have been expanded to explore other features of discourse, for example, devices of cohesion and coherence, modal verbs, hedges, politeness features, and so on. It might even have explored the CR problems arising in translation and interpretation (Burrough-Boenisch, 1998). While it is undeniably true that a book must have pages, it is also true that a book cannot exceed some rational number of pages—partly because the technology of bookbinding remains limited, and partly because publishing costs would soon exceed practical limits. What the world may need is a new massive multicultural corpus base where the problems can be explored beyond the limitations of any single focal point. In the absence of such a massive corpus, readers will find this volume a valuable introduction to the potential uses of CR in the composition classroom.

REFERENCES

Atkinson, D. (1999). *Scientific discourse in sociohistorical context: The Philosophical Transactions of the Royal Society of London, 1675–1975.* Mahwah, NJ: Lawrence Erlbaum Associates.

Baumgardner, R. (1987). Utilizing Pakistani newspaper English to teach grammar. *World Englishes, 6,* 241–252.

Baumgardner, R. (1992). 'To Shariat or not to Shariat?' Bilingual functional shifts in Pakistani English. *World Englishes, 11,* 129–140.

Berkenkotter, C., & Huckin, T. (1993). Rethinking genre from a sociocognitive perspective. *Written Communication, 10,* 475–509.

Berman, R., & Slobin, D. (Eds.). (1994). *Relating events in narrative: A crosslinguistic developmental study.* Hillsdale, NJ: Lawrence Erlbaum Associates.

Biber, D. (1988). *Variation across speech and writing.* Cambridge, England: Cambridge University Press.

Biber, D. (1992). On the complexity of discourse complexity: A multidimensional analysis. *Discourse Processes, 15,* 133–163.

Biber, D. (1995). *Cross-linguistic patterns of register variation: A multi-dimensional comparison of English, Tuvaluan, Korean, and Somali.* Oxford, England: Oxford University Press.

Bickner, R., & Peyasantiwong, P. (1988). Cultural variation in reflective writing. In A. Purves (Ed.), *Writing across languages and cultures* (pp. 160–174). Newbury Park, CA: Sage.

Bloch, J. (1989, July). *Toward a theory of contrastive rhetoric: The relationship between English and Chinese.* Paper presented at the Pennsylvania State Conference on Rhetoric and Composition.

Burrough-Boenisch, J. (1998). *Writing science like an English native speaker: How far can and should non-native speakers of English go?* Il Jornades Catalanes sobre Llengües per a Finalitats Específiques, Canet de Mar, Spain, Universitat de Barcelona.

Campbell, K. (1989, July). *Structural patterns in Chinese and English persuasive discourse.* Paper presented at the Pennsylvania State Conference on Rhetoric and Composition.

Cantor, S. (1994). *Writer involvement in abstract writing: An analysis of theme in English and Chinese abstracts.* Unpublished master's screening paper, Department of Linguistics, University of Southern California, Los Angeles.

Chang, S.-j. (1983). English and Korean. *Annual Review of Applied Linguistics, 3,* 85–98.

Cheng, P. (1985). *An analysis of contrastive rhetoric: English and Chinese expository prose, pedagogical implications, and strategies for the ESL teacher in a ninth grade curriculum.* Unpublished doctoral dissertation, Pennsylvania State University, University Park.

Chimombo, M. (1988, March). *Readability of subject texts: Implications for ESL teaching in Africa.* Paper presented at the annual TESOL Conference, Chicago.

Clyne, M. G. (1987). Cultural differences in the organization of academic texts: English and German. *Journal of Pragmatics, 11,* 211–247.

Connor, U. (1989). A contrastive study of persuasive business correspondence: American and Japanese. In S. J. Bruno (Ed.), *Global implications for business communications: Theory, technology, and practice.* Houston, TX: University of Houston–Clear Lake, School of Business and Public Administration.

Connor, U. (1996). *Contrastive rhetoric: Cross-cultural aspects of second-language writing.* New York: Cambridge University Press.

Dantas-Whitney, M., & Grabe, W. (1992). *A comparison of Portuguese and English newspaper editorials.* Flagstaff: Northern Arizona University.

Daoud, M. (1991). *The process of EST discourse: Arabic and French native speakers' recognition of rhetorical relationships in engineering texts.* Unpublished doctoral dissertation, University of California, Los Angeles.

Dellinger, B. (in press). Using the lacuna to detect implicitness in commercial news broadcasts. In H. Schröder (Ed.), *Lacunaology: Studies in intercultural communication.* Munich: Iudicium Verlag.

Dunkleblau, H. S. (1990). *A contrastive study of the organizational structure and stylistic elements of Chinese and English expository texts by Chinese high school students.* Unpublished paper.

Eggington, W. G. (1990). Contrastive analysis of Aboriginal English prose. In W. Walton & W. Eggington (Eds.), *Language: Maintenance, power and education in Australian Aboriginal contexts* (pp. 151–159). Darwin, Australia: Northern Territory University Press.

Enginarlar, H. (1990). *A contrastive analysis of writing in Turkish and English of Turkish high school students.* Unpublished doctoral dissertation, Hacettepe University, Turkey.

Enkvist, N. E. (1997). Why we need contrastive rhetoric. *Alternation, 4,* 188–206.

Ferris, D. (1991). *Syntactic and lexical characteristics of ESL student writing: A multidimensional study.* Unpublished doctoral dissertation, University of Southern California, Los Angeles.

Ferris, D. (1992). *Cross-cultural variation in ESL students' responses to an essay prompt.* Sacramento: California State University.

Ferris, D. (1993). The design of an automatic analysis program for L2 text research: Necessity and feasibility. *Journal of Second Language Writing, 2,* 119–129.

Ferris, D. (1994a). Lexical and syntactic features of ESL writing by students at different levels of proficiency. *TESOL Quarterly, 28,* 414–420.

Ferris, D. (1994b). Rhetorical strategies in student persuasive writing: Differences between native and non-native English speakers. *Research in the Teaching of English, 28,* 45–65.

Ferris, D., & Hedgcock, J. S. (1998). *Teaching ESL composition: Purpose, process, and practice.* Mahwah, NJ: Lawrence Erlbaum Associates.

Folman, S., & Connor, U. (1992, March). *Intercultural rhetorical differences in composing a research paper.* Paper presented at the International Teachers of English to Speakers of Other Languages Conference, Vancouver, Canada.

Folman, S., & Sarig, G. (1990). Intercultural rhetorical differences in meaning construction. *Communication and Cognition, 23,* 45–92.

Grabe, W., & Kaplan, R. B. (1996). *Theory and practice of writing: An applied linguistic perspective.* London: Longman.

Halliday, M. A. K. (1978). *Language as a social semiotic: The social interpretation of language and meaning.* London: Edward Arnold.

Hatim, B. (1991). The pragmatics of argumentation in Arabic: The rise and fall of a text type. *TEXT, 11,* 189–199.

Hinds, J. (1987). Reader versus writer responsibility. In U. Connor & R. B. Kaplan (Eds.), *Writing across languages: Analysis of L2 text* (pp. 141–152). Reading, MA: Addison-Wesley.

Hinds, J. (1990). Inductive, deductive, quasi-inductive: Expository writing in Japanese, Korean, Chinese and Thai. In U. Connor & A. Johns (Eds.), *Coherence in writing: Research and pedagogical perspectives.* Alexandria, VA: TESOL.

Indrasutra, C. (1988). Narrative styles in the writing of Thai and American students. In A. Purves (Ed.), *Writing across languages and cultures* (pp. 206–226). Newbury Park, CA: Sage.

Kachru, Y. (1983). English and Hindi. *Annual Review of Applied Linguistics, 3,* 78–84.

Kamhi-Stein, L. (1995). *The effect of strategy instruction on the summarization strategies of native speakers of Spanish in university-level general education courses.* Unpublished doctoral dissertation, University of Southern California, Los Angeles.

Kaplan, R. B. (1966). Cultural thought patterns in intercultural education. *Language Learning, 16,* 1–20.

Kaplan, R. B. (Ed.). (1995). The teaching of writing in the Pacific Basin [Special issue]. *Journal of Asian Pacific Communication, 6*(1&2).

Kaplan, R. B. (1997). Is there a problem in writing and reading texts across languages? In M. Pütz (Ed.), *The cultural context in foreign language teaching* (pp. 19–34). Frankfurt am Main: Peter Lang.

Kaplan, R. B. (in press-a). Contrastive rhetoric and discourse analysis: Who writes what to whom? when? under what circumstances? In R. M. Coulthard & S. Sarangi (Eds.), *Discourse and social life.* London: Longman.

Kaplan, R. B. (in press-b). English—The accidental language of science? In U. Ammon (Ed.), *Effects of the dominance of English as a language of science on the non-English language communities.* Berlin: Mouton deGruyter.

Kaplan, R. B. (in press-c). Why is English a global language? Problems and perplexities. In C. S. Ward (Ed.), *Selected papers from the 1999 RELC seminar.* Singapore: Regional Language Centre.

Kaplan, R. B., et al. (Eds.). (1983). *Annual Review of Applied Linguistics, 3.*

Kellerman, E. (1995). Crosslinguistic influence: Transfer to nowhere. *Annual Review of Applied Linguistics, 15,* 125–150.

Kowal, K. (1994, March). *Contrastive rhetoric and rhetorical theory: Some prolegomena to an eclectic philosophy of language.* Paper presented at the CCCC Conference, Chicago.

Leap, W. L. (1983). English and Native American languages. *Annual Review of Applied Linguistics, 3,* 24–37.

Lux, P. (1991). *Discourse styles of Anglo and Latin American college student writers.* Unpublished doctoral dissertation, Arizona State University, Tempe.

Lux, P., & Grabe, W. (1991). Multivariate approaches to contrastive rhetoric. *Lenguas Modernas, 18,* 133–160.

Manoliu-Manea, M. (1995). *Discourse and pragmatic constraints on grammatical choices: A grammar of surprises.* Amsterdam: Elsevier.

Mauranen, A. (1993). *Cultural differences in academic rhetoric* (Scandinavian University Studies in the Humanities and Social Sciences, Vol. 4). Frankfurt am Main: Peter Lang.

Montaño-Harmon, M. (1988). *Discourse features in the compositions of Mexican, English as a second language, Mexican-American/Chicano and Anglo high school students: Considerations for the formulation of educational policies.* Unpublished doctoral dissertation, University of Southern California, Los Angeles.

Montaño-Harmon, M. (1991). Discourse features of written Mexican Spanish: Current research in contrastive rhetoric and its implications. *Hispania, 74,* 417–425.

Moulton, W. G. (1963). *The sounds of English and German.* Chicago: University of Chicago Press.

Neustupny, J. V. (1997, November). Teaching communication or teaching interaction? *Chiba University Journal,* 1–13.

Oi, K., & Sato, T. (1990). Cross-cultural rhetorical differences in letter writing: Refusal letter and application letter. *Daigaku eigo kyoiku gakukai,* 117–136.

Oktar, L. (1991). *A contrastive analysis of specific rhetorical relations in English and Turkish expository paragraph writing.* Unpublished doctoral dissertation, Ege University, Turkey.

Ostler, S. E. (1987). English in parallels: A comparison of English and Arabic prose. In U. Connor & R. B. Kaplan (Eds.), *Writing across languages: Analysis of L2 text* (pp. 169–185). Reading, MA: Addison-Wesley.

Ostler, S. E. (1992). *Cultural sensitivities: Teaching Spanish speakers to write in English.* Bowling Green, OH: Bowling Green University.

Pandharipanda, R. (1983). English and Marathi. *Annual Review of Applied Linguistics, 3,* 118–136.

Ramanathan, V., & Kaplan, R. B. (2000). *Genres, authors, discourse communities: Theory and application for L2 teacher-training.* Manuscript in preparation. (A version of this paper was presented at the TESOL Conference, Seattle, 1998)

Reid, J. (1988). *Quantitative differences in English prose written by Arabic, Chinese, Spanish, and English students.* Unpublished doctoral dissertation, Colorado State University, Ft. Collins.

Reppen, R., & Grabe, W. (1993). Spanish transfer effects in the English writing of elementary school students. *Lenguas Modernas, 20,* 113–128.

Sa'Adeddin, M. A. (1987). Target world experiential matching: The Arabic–English translating case. *Quinquireme, 10,* 137–164.

Sa'Adeddin, M. A. (1989). Text development and Arabic–English negative interference. *Applied Linguistics, 10,* 36–51.

Scollon, R. (1991, March). *Eight legs and one elbow: Stance and structure in Chinese English compositions.* Paper presented at the International Reading Association Second North American Conference on Adult and Adolescent Literacy, Banff, Canada.

Scollon, R. (1997). Contrastive rhetoric, contrastive poetics, or perhaps something else? *TESOL Quarterly, 31,* 352–358.

Skyum-Nielsen, P., & Schröder, H. (Eds.). (1994). *Rhetoric and stylistics today.* Frankfurt am Main: Peter Lang.

Soter, A. (1988). The second language learner and cultural transfer in narration. In A. Purves (Ed.), *Writing across languages and cultures* (pp. 378–388). Newbury Park, CA: Sage.

Stockwell, R. P., & Bowen, J. D. (1965). *The sounds of English and Spanish.* Chicago: University of Chicago Press.

Stockwell, R. P., & Martin, J. W. (1965). *The grammatical structures of English and Spanish*. Chicago: University of Chicago Press.

Trueba, H. T. (1986). Bilingualism and bilingual education (1984–1985). *Annual Review of Applied Linguistics, 6*, 47–64.

Tsao, F.-f. (1983). Linguistics and writing in particular languages: English and Chinese. *Annual Review of Applied Linguistics, 3*, 99–117.

Ulijn, J. M., & Strother, J. B. (1995). *Communicating in business and technology: From psycholinguistic theory to international practice*. Frankfurt am Main: Peter Lang.

Villanueva, V. (1995). *Bootstraps: From an American academic of color*. Urbana, IL: National Council of Teachers of English.

Weasenforth, D. (1995). *Rhetorical abstraction as a facet of expected response: A structural equation modeling analysis*. Unpublished doctoral dissertation, University of Southern California, Los Angeles.

Wijst, P. van der, & Ulijn, J. M. (1995). Politeness in French/Dutch negotiations: The linguistic realization of politeness strategies. In K. Ehlich & J. Wagner (Eds.), *The discourse of business negotiations* (pp. 313–348). Berlin: Mouton deGruyter.

Youmans, M. (1995). *Communicative rights and responsibilities in an East Los Angeles barrio: An analysis of epistemic modal use*. Unpublished doctoral dissertation, University of Southern California, Los Angeles.

Preface

Clayann Gilliam Panetta
Christian Brothers University

Contrastive rhetoric has interested me throughout graduate school and be-yond because it provides an avenue to explore *why* we all make the rhetorical decisions we do. Over the years it has occurred to me that contrastive rheto-ric has larger and broader implications, namely, that it can be applied to a wide range of cultural differences in addition to the English-as-a-second-language (ESL) issues for which it was originally created. This volume is the first step toward making this realization a reality, bringing to the forefront a number of different and newer ways to visualize contrastive rhetoric for the rhetoric and composition classroom. In doing so, my aim is to breathe new life into con-trastive rhetoric for rhetoric and composition instructors.

The chapters in this volume are divided into two parts. In the first, I have invited linguists as well as rhetoric and composition instructors to demonstrate ways in which contrastive rhetoric can be useful for supporting ESL students in a rhetoric and composition class. In the second, I have invited contributions from other "difference" groups, who offer suggestions for using contrastive rhet-oric as a stepping-stone toward a widespread cultural understanding of rhetori-cal decisions. By bringing together these two groups of chapters, my hope is that rhetoric and composition instructors will see contrastive rhetoric as vital to their pedagogy. Clearly, both parts of this volume serve simply as a taste of how contrastive rhetoric can be revisited and redefined for rhetoric and composition classes. My aim is to start a conversation in this vein, a conversation that now has the potential to take a number of different directions.

I must thank several people who have been instrumental in bringing this project to reality. First, my family: Carl Panetta, my husband, who has almost as much pride in my work as I do and doesn't mind telling people so; Anna Clay Panetta, my daughter, whose smiles and giggles have helped me under-stand when rhetorical contrasts begin; and Clay and Nelda Gilliam, my parents, without whose support I would not have pursued projects like this one. I must also acknowledge Fred Reynolds, my constant advisor, whose words of encouragement and direction have guided me even when I didn't know I needed guiding, and Bob Kaplan, whose advice and guidance have made this project cleaner and better for the intended audience.

Most important, I must thank my contributors, who have not only done a splendid job of writing about contrastive rhetoric, but who have given it new life, a life that should begin new conversations and project ideas for instructors and graduate students in rhetoric and composition.

One editorial note: Readers will notice two referential inconsistencies in this volume. First, some contributors prefer "contrastive rhetoric" over "contrastive rhetoric theory," and vice versa. Second, contributors refer to speakers for whom English is their second language in a number of different ways (ESL, L2, etc.). I have decided to keep these inconsistencies intact both to protect individual rhetorical preferences and to demonstrate the basic argument of this book—that rhetorical choices have purposeful roots.

I

CONTRASTIVE RHETORIC REVISITED

1

Understanding Cultural Differences in the Rhetoric and Composition Classroom: Contrastive Rhetoric as Answer to ESL Dilemmas[1]

Clayann Gilliam Panetta
Christian Brothers University

Contrastive rhetoric—the term used to describe the argument that the linguistical, organizational, and presentational choices that English-as-a-second-language (ESL) student-writers make substantively differ from the choices that native-English student-writers make—has only relatively recently been prominent in the scholarly literature and teacher-talk of composition. The whole notion of a "contrastive rhetoric" began in 1966 with Robert Kaplan, who, along with other writing instructors, discovered that the writing patterns of international students who had recently come to the United States were much different from the writing patterns of native writers. He began research into these phenomena, examining the writing of ESL students and trying to determine where their writing deviated from that of native users of English. By closely analyzing compositions written by ESL students, he realized that the differences he had noted were not simply grammatical or surface matters (differences in "spelling . . . or differences in lexicon"), but underlying differences, including "paragraph order and structure" (Kaplan, 1988, p. 277). He then compared ESL cultural practices to typical Western practices and found many

---

[1]Portions of this chapter also appeared in my *College ESL* article "Contrastive Rhetoric in Technical Writing Pedagogy at Urban Institutions" (Panetta, 1997).

3

interesting rhetorical trends and deviations (Piper, 1985). Student-writers from Anglo-European languages seemed to prefer linear developments, whereas student-writers from Asian languages seemed to take a more indirect approach, coming to their points at the ends of their papers. The paragraph development in writing done by students from Semitic languages tended to be based on a series of parallel organizations of coordinate, rather than subordinate, clauses, whereas students from Romance and Russian languages tended to prefer extraneous material (Connor, 1996). In short, Kaplan was able to suggest that rhetorical structure is not universal, but culture-dependent (Piper, 1985).

Kaplan coined the phrase *contrastive rhetoric* to describe the differences he had seen, and he began to encourage instructors to use his research in their classrooms (Purves, 1988). To aid these instructors, he created diagrams to explain the five different types of paragraph development he had identified.[2] His aim in this compilation was, first, to help ESL students better understand the typical patterning of English rhetoric by contrasting it to the rhetorical patterning of their culture. He also encouraged close instructor scrutiny of contrastive rhetoric, because contrastive rhetoric would be a pedagogical contributor to reading and writing issues—more advanced ESL reading and writing students could be taught about language characteristics and differences among cultures (Piper, 1985). Kaplan saw this as vital information to any instructor of ESL; understanding the rhetorical deviations apparent in languages would bridge the gap between cultural encoding and decoding. In essence, instructors were called to realize that "differences among rhetorical patterns do not represent differences in cognitive ability, but differences in cognitive style" (Purves, 1988, p. 19).

Li (1996) has shown this to be true in the following discourse:

> I was considered a good writer in China. . . . I still remember the "appreciation classes," during which the teacher read aloud to the class a number of the best student papers from the last assignment and analyzed the accomplishments of each selected piece. . . . I remember the pride and joy when my writing was read to the class, and the secret comparison I made with the selected papers when they were read. The climax usually came at the end of the class when the teacher walked down the aisles and handed us our papers with grades and her written comments. Although I often had more or less the same comments—"Well-structured, fluent and expressive use of language . . ."—I cherished the red lines scribbled on my paper, for the teacher was talking to me about my writing, alone. . . .
>
> In my American classes I soon found myself struggling aimlessly. . . . The problem was not with grammar or the lexicon . . . , supposedly the most daunted aspects of English for a Chinese learner, for although I did have many problems with the linguistic aspect of the language, I could always consult grammar books and dic-

---

[2]See Kaplan (1966).

tionaries, and I was used to doing that. It was comments beyond the sentence level in my writing that left me in endless speculation. The instructions were usually kind and encouraging, telling me that I should write "just what you think," and write in my "honest voice." But other comments indicated that to write just what I think and in the way that I felt most comfortable were not good enough. My writing was sometimes "too vague," other times "lacked specifics," and still others "redundant," or I was told that I should "go straight to the point." I was at a loss as to how to be "specific" yet not "redundant," how to avoid "beating around the bush" and to be subtle and suggestive (aren't they the same?), and more important, what was worth writing. (p. xi)

The difficulty Li notes is characteristic of most ESL students in American writing classes; Kaplan's aim was to answer such dilemmas.

Over subsequent decades, contrastive rhetoric has gathered both proponents and opposition. Proponents have touted the pedagogical implications of contrastive rhetoric. For instance, Leki (1991) pointed out that even though writing instructors who teach ESL students may not have backgrounds in the rhetorics of different cultures, contrastive rhetoric helps us bypass stereotypes and realize that writing strategies are culturally formed (p. 138). For example, what is relevant/irrelevant, what is logical/illogical, what constitutes an argument, even, are all *culturally* determined. Sometimes ESL writers seem to "miss the point." However, the "proper" way to make a point in one language differs from the "proper" way in another (Leki, 1992). Pointing out and realizing such contrasts between rhetorics helps instructors and students analyze what represents successful communication among cultures. As Purves (1988) pointed out, "When students, taught to write in one culture, enter another and do not write as do the members of the second culture, they should not be thought stupid or lacking in 'higher mental processes,' as some composition teachers have stated" (p. 19). Instead, they simply do not know about the rhetorical structures of the new culture, but they have the capability to learn the new conventions if given ample opportunity (p. 19). In short, a number of researchers have argued that, with contrastive rhetoric, instructors who teach writing to ESL students can come to see that *our* truth is not *the* truth and that, in reality, truth is a relative concept across cultures and languages (Leki, 1991).

On the other hand, Kaplan has been accused by some of "reductionism—of trying to reduce the whole of linguistics to this single issue" (Kaplan, 1987, p. 9). Others have added that his observations were faulty because he focused on English but implicated other languages (p. 10). Furthermore, since Kaplan's diagrams for language characteristics were so simplistic, Leki (1992) has shown that many teachers and students have come to think of rhetorical patterns as *equal* to native thought patterns of other cultures. However, strategies for successful communication are not innate or universal; they are rhetorical. For instance, one study has shown how the goal of the ancient Chinese rhetorical tradition differs from the goal of the Western rhetorical tradition. Instead of using rhetoric to "convince political equals in a public forum of some political position, placing a great deal of emphasis on an individual speaker's ability to reason and to marshal proofs," the Asian tradition called on the rhetor to "announce truth. . . . Language was used not to discover but to uncover truth based on accepted traditional wisdom" (Leki, 1992, pp. 89–90). At the same time, politically, "lack of clarity . . . helped the ruling elite retain power" (pp. 89–90). They confused the audience to remind the audience of the rhetor's superiority. Examples like these show how contrasting rhetorics represent historical, social, economic, and political issues, "not natural mental processes or psychological capabilities" (pp. 89–90), as Kaplan initially indicated. Finally, others have criticized Kaplan's disregard for Aristotelian rhetoric in two ways. First, he truncated the canons from invention, arrangement, style, memory, and delivery to only arrangement; second, he excluded persuasion from his view of rhetoric (Connor, 1997, p. 32).

Kaplan (1987) agreed with some of this criticism, admitting that, "in the first blush of discovery, [he] overstated both the differences[s] and [his] case" (p. 9).[3] Nevertheless, he does not "regret having made the case." To Kaplan, "[the] issue is that each language has clear preferences, so that while all forms are possible, all forms do not occur with equal frequency or in parallel distributions" (p. 11). Native writers have at their disposal a number of rhetorical alternatives, but non-native writers do not posses this inventory and do not know about the sociolinguistic constraints on the alternatives. Pedagogically, our job should be to increase this inventory (Kaplan, 1987). One way this has been done, according to Connor (1997), has been to revise the contrastive rhetoric paradigm and definition to reflect the broader implications of contrastive rhetoric: "A broader definition that considers cognitive and sociocultural variables of writing in addition to linguistic variables has been substituted for a purely linguistic framework interested in structural analyses of products" (pp. 18–19). In short, Connor continues, "Contrastive rhetoric has moved from examining only products to studying processes in a variety of writing situations" (pp. 18–19).[4] Therefore, some have argued that if writing instructors avoid the reductionist tendencies of contrastive rhetoric and use it as a way of realizing the tremendous role culture plays in ESL students' rhetorics, then it can become a powerful resource for conquering the difficult ESL (and other "difference") issues that present themselves in all rhetoric and composition classes.

---

[3]He even began to refer to the article in which he first presented the diagrams that represented different cultural patterns as his "doodles article."
[4]This book is a part of this broader definition and hopes to look further into cultural differences in general in the rhetoric and composition classroom. Some contributors here even argue that the basic principles of contrastive rhetoric theory are applicable to a wider range of cultural differences.

The increasing need for specific training in American rhetorical styles is a responsibility that does *inevitably* fall on writing instructors because it is in writing classes that one would expect culturally based rhetorical differences to most readily present themselves. Unfortunately, as Dillon (1992) pointed out, many writing instructors, who are "hired to teach all students how to use language effectively," simply feel ill-equipped for teaching ESL students:

> To teach English as a second language . . . , he or she has to know something about students' first languages, but the typical nonheterogeneous mix of L2 learners renders impractical, if not impossible, attempts to discover or design an appropriate variety of learning aids. . . . [S]pecialists who are not formally trained to teach English to speakers of other languages get unnecessarily mired in philosophical misgivings, suffering guilt because they are less adept at hurdling the language barrier than are the students whose "errors" they judge. (p. 9)

Fortunately, contrastive rhetoric can give instructors avenues to get over this barrier. Furthermore, given its emphasis on teaching students American rhetorical patterns (and, to a lesser extent, exposing American students to such patterns), contrastive rhetoric ought almost naturally to be of special interest to teachers of rhetoric and composition.

Some have argued, though, that rhetoric and composition has its own discourse patterns that even native writers must learn, and that contrastive rhetoric may not be *the* key to ESL writing instruction. However, it is because of these patterns that contrastive rhetoric is *most* applicable to composition. For example, when several Japanese writing students were asked to describe good writing, they described it as writing that "would engage the emotions through beauty, surprise, and flow" (Leki, 1992, p. 98). Of course, native writers would see writing more as a tool, not as an object with aesthetic value. The same students' approach to audience also showed notable contrasts. While their U.S. counterparts' main concerns were on audience, and they worked to "ensure that their argument would be adequately hedged, that their position would remain fairly unassailable, and that the user/reader of the text would understand it" (pp. 98–99), the Japanese worked

> to make the text aesthetically acceptable. . . . Furthermore, they felt that writing was not a discovery process at all but rather that writing should come only *after* thinking (that is writing itself is not used in order to think more clearly). If a new idea occurred to these writers during the writing, they ignored it and did not try to find a way to incorporate it. (pp. 98–99)

Clearly, the "mistakes" the ESL students were making were beyond the surface level. It should be paramount for composition instructors to clarify patterns like these to ESL students, and a contrastive rhetoric focus could facilitate that process.

Unfortunately, contrastive rhetoric appears to be yet another composition theory that has not made its way into mainstream teaching—a finding that, at the very least, dramatically confirms Welch's (1987) argument that composition practice is "theory-unconscious" (p. 269). One could argue, of course, that instructors who do not incorporate contrastive rhetoric into their pedagogy really are not atheoretical, that other approaches to writing could have taken precedence over their references to contrastive rhetoric. Perhaps this is true. However, given its direct applicability to composition and the constant globalization of academia, contrastive rhetoric must begin to exist *alongside* any other theoretical stances in the writing class. Therefore, writing instructors need only add contrastive rhetoric to their pedagogy, not replace another theory.

Adding onto one's pedagogy is often difficult; however, incorporating contrastive rhetoric is not as intrusive as it initially seems. Many instructors argue that they do not have time to learn about other cultures' rhetorical preferences. Yes, it is helpful to learn about other cultural traditions and point out contrasts to students in our classes, but even without having done that, instructors can incorporate contrastive rhetoric through the same strategies they already use. What should be added to these familiar strategies is simply a contrastive rhetoric foundation, and this can be accomplished by making Western writing conventions explicit. In what follows I share some strategies I have found useful in making writing conventions explicit in both traditional composition classes and in business/technical writing classes.[5]

MAKING WRITING CONVENTIONS EXPLICIT

Although most writing instructors take pride in their ability to make their assignments explicit, the rhetorical tendencies of ESL students call on us to take some extra time to recognize the special needs of those ESL students. As a Western writer and teacher, I have learned not to take understanding for granted in a diverse classroom.[6]

As researchers into contrastive rhetoric have shown, writers often use the writing conventions with which they are most comfortable, but the rhetorical choices ESL students have learned in their culture may not be effective for American compositions. By using the following example of the digressive tendencies of Brazilian writers, we can see how this can be true:

> *There is something difficult about being in a different culture, or just speaking a foreign language; that is "appropriateness." In my opinion that is one of the hardest issues in*

---

[5]Although I do not suggest that these pedagogical strategies are the only ways to incorporate contrastive rhetoric into a writing class, they have been the most successful for me, and they serve here as starting points for other writing instructors to begin to incorporate contrastive rhetoric pedagogically.

[6]Consequently, even my Anglo students have benefited from such clarity.

coping with differences. When is the right time to say "hello," or "hi," or start a conversation? When to ask personal questions or just be indifferent? When and under what circumstances is it appropriate to do such and such? Basically, human beings are the same, and have more or less the same potential attitudes, knowledge and skills, so why are they so diverse? I think that what changes is the composition of the different elements or the way they are structured based on facts and circumstances. For instance, Americans say "Time is money," and money in a capitalist system is something to be saved or invested in productivity. It sounds crazy, but I think this idea can change the whole concept of time and the way it is spent in a society. Time and space are two abstract concepts that are lived by the way they are defined. I do not know what comes first, the system, the cultural values, or the people, but whatever order they have, they seem to be interrelated somehow. So if I have to make a stereotype of how American culture appears to me, I would say it is rational, dry, left-brain oriented, individualistic, values individual initiative and individual freedom, self-centered and proud of itself.
The third time I came to the U.S. . . . . (Fox, 1994, p. 20)

When Fox (1994) discussed this writing style with a student, she found that Brazilian writing is "characteristically [a] digressive style of expression." Furthermore, "the writer does not necessarily feel the weight of responsibility to 'make sense'" (p. 21). Instead, the audience must do the communicative analysis and derive meaning from the discourse, and the writer's task is to give the meaning in several different ways so that the reader finally gets the message the writer aims to convey (p. 21). In the words of Brazilian students in general: "You don't want to depress your audience by giving everything away immediately . . . , leaving nothing for them to do. And you don't want to bore them, either, so you do what is considered interesting, which is to give plenty of details and a conversational tone to your written text" (p. 22). Once an instructor finds out these things, the instructor can explain how this approach differs from Western rhetoric, where we are taught to be "specific," "clear," and "precise," and that digressive details are "unacceptable" in the Western definition of literate culture.

In an example from Tony, an Angolan student, we can again see that cultural *practices* play a role in the rhetorical choices students make when they write:

I agree and I believe most people do, that one should marry whom he or she loves. Yet, if the couple were from different races, many would disagree with me. For instance, Malcolm X, in his autobiography refers to the relationship between mixed couples as being entirely sexual, lacking in love and with complete disrespect between partners. This is the idea most Americans have regarding interracial marriage. (Fox, 1994, p. 31)

In this case, Tony's instructor questioned Tony's generalizing "all Americans." However, as the instructor soon discovered, in Angola when a famous person speaks, he speaks for everyone: "When a filmmaker makes a movie, or someone speaks at a public assembly, they are saying what the whole society believes" (p. 31). After knowing this, the instructor explained to Tony that

American culture is more individualistic: When Spike Lee makes a film, we see that as Spike Lee's opinion, not necessarily the society's as a whole (Fox, 1994, p. 31).

Technical/business writing classes also often require similar attention to ESL students' rhetorical choices in their assignments. To demonstrate, notice the differences between the following two progress reports (a common assignment in such classes) written by Asian employees:

> 3. *I changed the code to do error recovery when slct1 returns -4 and I also worked with John to look into the interface between dumper and response translator.*
> 4. *I attended several meetings and the talk given by Ann _____. There are still quite a lot to work on.*

> *I received a new assignment by my new boss in the new year. The assignment is to maintain the survey-routine. Is it fun to maintain some one else code? Well, now I am doing that so if any one has any problems with survey—please contact me and don't bother the original author. Mary has explained the design of the routine to me (thinks mary I know you have very busy schedule) and it took a day or two to understand the code. Susan assigned all the pending code changes (four of them) for the survey—to me on Friday and I fixed them over the weekend. I was very happy, but on Monday when I was testing the code I discovered an interesting problem with on of the code changes. . . .*
> *I discovered that the same thing was happening if there were more then eight . . . It took me a day to find out why it was happening and this time there was a big problem. The algorithm for a function called . . . was wrong so I redesign and recorded the algorithm. Louise and I also discovered that LL . . . had wrong constants (thanks Louise).* (Belcher, 1991, pp. 111–112)

Progress reports are, of course, used to make one's accomplishments known and are obvious opportunities for self-promotion. However, contrastive rhetoricians argue that Asians are not accustomed to thinking of themselves in terms of their individual achievements (Belcher, 1991, p. 112). The first progress-report example shows this. The second one, written by an Asian employee who has learned to express himself according to "American" progress-report protocols (using a discursive approach, focusing on a significant problem solved, mentioning the roles of fellow employees and their supervisor), is notably different. It comes across as having been written by someone who is not only a hard-working and clear-thinking employee, but also a gregarious and grateful one. The writer also appears quite satisfied with the job and is appreciative of other colleagues. Even though there are still language-use errors, there is an attempt to establish rapport through the inclusion of colleagues. Research has shown that native writers may be more accepting of grammatical problems if rapport is established in the writing (Belcher, 1991, p. 112). Instructors of technical/business writing need to clarify these differences to their students.

Through examples like these, we can see that if we discuss with ESL students the reasons they make the choices they do, we can gain some understanding of students' native rhetorical choices, bridging rhetorical gaps so writer, instructor, and even peer reader have a common ground from which to work with and on the writing. Most important, this knowledge can open up avenues for the instructor to make the assignment more explicit to ESL writers.[7]

At the same time, ESL students need not be taught that there is only one "American" approach to writing. Just as a variety of writing conventions must exist in their culture, a variety of conventions are available and expected in Western rhetoric, so if students learn the conventions appropriate to only one genre, we are doing them a tremendous disservice. For instance, first-year composition often touts itself as the precursor to "all writing you will do in college," so ESL students, who struggle with the language (both in translation and through the cultural issues we have been discussing), attempt to apply the same writing standards to all writing assignments they receive after having passed first-year composition. However, not all assignments will reflect the instruction they received in first-year composition, and they need to be told that.

In technical/business writing classes, for example, students learn specific conventions for specific types of writing (various letter forms, job application information, various report forms, memos, minutes, etc.), often a deviation (in their mind's eye) from what they are taught in first-year composition.

A technical-writing ESL student commented to me once that he had discovered that he had been able to be "more colorful" in his writing in his first-year composition class when he wrote about an experience. But technical writing has lesser liberties for digressions, causing him to struggle with which exact things should be included in a document and which things he should avoid. (Most of the time his instructor met with him and marked out his digressions, but he feared that after graduation he would not be able to read his writing as critically and make those revision decisions for himself.) In essence, while he had noticed the differences between the genres once the instructor had finished marking his paper, the student still did not understand *why* the differences existed. He had learned not to digress in first-year composition, but *some* amount of digression had been acceptable to his first-year composition instructor. However, technical writing allowed for *no* digressions, leaving the student confused about writing in English altogether. Instruction on when certain stylistic decisions are correct and *why* they are correct, according to genre, would have been most helpful for this student.

---

[7]Once I learn something about a culture in this way I am more attuned to that culture's preferences, causing me to make the conventions associated with certain assignments clear to *everyone* in my class when I make the assignment in the first place.

Leki (1991) has shown that "readers understand and recall better what they are familiar with and expect" (p. 103). Thus, writing instructors are responsible for teaching English audience expectations, helping ESL students "increase the perceived quality of their texts" (p. 103). Therefore, if instructors of writing clarify how the rhetoric necessary for the audiences emphasized in their class differs from the rhetoric emphasized to other audiences, ESL students (and native writers as well) could easily overcome what was once a tremendous barrier.

CONCLUSION

The pedagogical implications of these realizations are critical; as Leki (1992) reiterated, they help "both teacher and student analyze the quality of texts that are admired and considered to represent successful communication" (p. 138). Furthermore,

> students who are having trouble writing in English and who are made aware of cultural differences in rhetoric suddenly view themselves, not as suffering from individual inadequacies, but as coming from a particular rhetorical tradition, which they must retain of course, but which cannot be applied wholesale to English writing. (p. 138)

When writing instructors incorporate contrastive rhetoric into their pedagogy, they help writing students realize differences between "foreign" and "American" rhetorics and pave the way for better communication. In short, if ESL students learn about rhetorical differences, then they learn about situations that might call for a rhetoric different from theirs. They learn that their native rhetoric is not wrong, just ineffective for American readers. (Similarly, if students representing other "difference" groups learned about rhetorical differences, they too might shift from right/wrong stances to more productive effective/ineffective stances.[8]) This chapter has opened discussion into how to facilitate this process through a focus on making writing conventions explicit. Such learning matters, and the most logical place for it to take place is in the writing classroom.

REFERENCES

Belcher, D. (1991). Nonnative writing in a corporate setting. *The Technical-Writing Teacher, 18,* 104–115.

Connor, U. M. (1996). Contrastive rhetoric. In T. Enos (Ed.), *Encyclopedia of rhetoric and composition* (pp. 146–148). New York: Garland.

---

[8]See Bliss (chap. 2), Corbett (chap. 3), Micciche (chap. 6), and Comfort (chap. 7), this volume.

Connor, U. M. (1997). *Contrastive rhetoric*. Cambridge, England: Cambridge University Press.

Dillon, W. T. (1992). Nuclear sentences: Teaching cohesion to L2 business writers. *The Bulletin, 1*, 9–15.

Fox, H. (1994). *Listening to our world*. Urbana, IL: National Council of Teachers of English.

Kaplan, R. (1966). Cultural thought patterns in inter-cultural education. *Language Learning, 16*, 1–20.

Kaplan, R. (1987). Cultural thought patterns revisited. In R. Kaplan & U. Connor (Eds.), *Writing across languages: Analysis of L2 text* (pp. 9–22). Reading, MA: Addison-Wesley.

Kaplan, R. (1988). Contrastive rhetoric and second language learning: Notes toward a theory of contrastive rhetoric. In A. C. Purves (Ed.), *Writing across languages and cultures* (pp. 143–154). Beverly Hills, CA: Sage.

Leki, I. (1991). Twenty-five years of contrastive rhetoric: Text analysis and writing pedagogies. *TESOL Quarterly, 25*, 123–143.

Leki, I. (1992). *Understanding ESL writers: A guide for teachers*. Portsmouth, NH: Heinemann.

Li, X.-M. (1996). *Good writing*. Albany: State University of New York Press.

Panetta, C. G. (1997). Contrastive rhetoric in technical-writing pedagogy at urban institutions. *College ESL, 7*, 70–80.

Piper, D. (1985). Contrastive rhetoric and reading in a second language: Theoretical perspectives on classroom practice. *Canadian Modern Language Review, 42*, 34–43.

Purves, A. C. (1988). Preface. *Writing across languages and cultures*. Beverly Hills, CA: Sage.

Welch, K. E. (1987). Ideology and freshman textbook production: The place of theory in writing pedagogy. *College Composition and Communication, 38*, 269–282.

2

Rhetorical Structures for Multilingual and Multicultural Students

Anne Bliss
University of Colorado, Boulder

Multicultural and multilingual students at the college and university level present diverse approaches to reading, writing, and critical thinking, often based in the patterns of their home languages and cultures. Frequently, these students may use different ways to convey ideas logically and persuasively than those with which native English-speaking faculty and students are familiar. Kennedy (1998) discussed textual "arrangement" of the type most used in American academic prose:

> "Arrangement" in traditional Western rhetoric concerns the division of a work into identifiable parts that perform specific functions: the "proemium" or introduction should get the attention, interest, and good will of the audience; the "narration" should provide the audience with background and necessary fact to understand the argument; the "proof" should identify the question at issue and the thesis, followed by supporting arguments. It may also refute the arguments of an opponent. The final part is the "epilogue," which should recapitulate the main points made earlier and stir the emotions of the audience to belief or action. (p. 7)

Multilingual and multicultural students may not present knowledge and ideas according to this typical academic pattern, and, as a result, they often find themselves and their written or spoken work either not understood or not accepted. As Hauser (1986) stated, "Insofar as our utterances are within the cultural framework of our audience, its members may participate actively in reconceptualizing their experiences in terms that we provide" (p. 146). When the cultural frame, as well as the language structure, differs between writer and audience, the interaction between reader and text, and the reconceptualization of the notions conveyed, may be skewed.

To communicate effectively in American college classes requires more than just words, pronunciation, syntax, or the desire to convey ideas. To persuade others of our intent and meaning, we depend on transactions between the speaker or writer and the audience, and on logical connections between ordered information sets. Yet, such rhetorical factors as indirectness, politeness, explicit statements, and so forth play a large role in much of the text generated by these students (Purves & Purves, 1986). Although it is possible to convey our ideas through these modes as well as through clean, graceful speaking or writing style, our rhetorical or persuasive power stems from the functions of the text itself. We, and our multicultural and multilingual students, depend on interpersonal, ideational, and textual transactions that are sequenced chronologically, psychologically, and rhetorically. Both theoretical and practical rhetorical strategies for patterning can help our university students develop logical connections that enable them to produce the types of prose required by the academy. In no way do I wish to undervalue or to change the traditional rhetorical structures that these students use; I wish instead to give them some extra tricks and some different structures that will enable them to communicate effectively through the traditionally expected and somewhat closed-minded prescriptive form or "arrangement" of Western academic rhetoric. I discuss rhetorical structures useful primarily in writing, but my remarks also pertain to reading, speaking, and critical listening.

In general, university faculty ask students to produce two types of writing: descriptive and persuasive. Examples of descriptive writing include the précis, summary, abstract, lab report, essay exam responses that inform the instructor about whether or not students have retained particular information, and descriptive research papers. We might also include descriptive writing within categories of creative writing or essays required for some classes. Descriptive writing tells "what": what something is or looks like, what happened in an experiment, what someone did, and so forth. Most of our multicultural students can handle descriptive writing fairly well, because the ordering of information leads to reader response in the form of images (rather than being persuaded), or to repetition of facts learned, or memorized, for an exam.

However, when our students are asked to write to inform or persuade, many of them have serious difficulties. Persuasive writing at the university level includes a variety of genres and formats that require students to develop an assertive thesis, one that makes a claim, and to support that thesis logically with substantive evidence. When multilingual and multicultural students are faced with such writing assignments, they may face logical and structural problems because they may not know how to connect their ideas and their evidence in the expected rhetorical structure. They may present discrete bits of information that seem disconnected or not even related to the thesis. Or, they may present a kind of story or analogy as a way to explain their point of view. In many cases, these students rely on their native cultural and linguistic patterns of explanation, and, as a result, to their instructors, their writing seems disorganized and neither informative nor persuasive.

Linguists working with comparative and contrastive rhetoric (Kaplan, 1987; Kennedy, 1998) recognize that the underlying structures of all languages are not alike. Empirically we know that ourselves, from working with students whose cultural variations work with their native languages to form what I call the "list discrete points in order to inform" languages, the "think along with me even if I don't tell you the answer" languages, and the "storytelling without providing the moral or logical conclusion" languages. In Japanese, for example, it is typically considered rude to point out to the listener or reader what that person should believe or do. Yet, academic English often demands an overt statement about what the reader should do or believe, followed by evidence that supports the writer's claim.

An example of the cultural and linguistic conflict can be seen in former President George Bush's visit to Japan several years ago when he appeared before the Japanese legislators and told them to buy American cars. Japanese newspapers, television, and people on the street remarked at the rudeness of the American President who was telling them what to do. Yet, if the President told us Americans that we should "buy American" we would most likely not think him rude; we might not like what he says, and we might disagree, but we would not attribute his remarks to rudeness.

After reports of the Japanese opinion reached American newspapers, commentators remarked that the Japanese did not understand Bush's intent, that he did not intend to be rude. Commentators also noted that if the Japanese didn't buy American cars or parts, Congress would probably cut Japan's automobile import levels. The perception of rudeness, and the American response, can, I believe, be at least partly attributed to underlying linguistic differences in the cultures and to the logical structures of Japanese and English. Although it is easy to give an order in Japanese, if one wants to persuade someone to do something, the speaker rarely tells that person what to do. Instead, the typical persuasive structure might mention discrete points favoring the proposition, and, after listening to these points, the listener will agree or disagree with the proposition—even though it has never been stated directly. To most English speakers, however, such a Japanese speaker seems to be "talking around" the proposition.

If President Bush had followed the discrete point structure, he would have mentioned factors such as American cars are strong, American cars are efficient, American cars have well-built engines, and so forth. And, by the end of his list, if his items were attractive, his listeners would have come to the conclusion that they ought to buy an American car.

Kaplan (1972) referred to *discourse units* as "units within a discourse bloc which are related to each other by either coordination, subordination, or superordination" (p. 270), in what he refers to as "agitated interaction" in three modes: "psychological, rhetorical, and grammatical" (p. 95). Although these systems of ordination and interaction enable English speakers and writers to provide meaning, speakers of other languages may not use or understand them. Bush's superordination of his request and the interaction of his ideas and support seemed offensive within culture and language that use different psychological, rhetorical, and grammatical structures. Our students may face similar situations when they present their writing to American faculty; the interaction may fail because the writer and reader fail to comprehend the arrangement of ideas.

The President followed the typical American academic rhetorical structure with an overtly stated thesis followed by support in the form of reasons and discrete details. He first stated, "You must buy American cars," and then he gave a few bits of supporting evidence about the cars and trade issues. His argument was linear; he immediately went straight to the heart of the issue and then offered evidence to bolster his claim. Although the discrete point structure may seem somewhat circular to us, as if someone is "beating around the bush," not getting to the point, the direct linear structure can violate cultural and linguistic norms.

A few additional examples might also help us understand the need for teaching our multicultural and multilingual university students about logical ordering. My Korean students sometimes tell me that English seems to be a very stupid language, implying, perhaps, that those of us who use English must not be very intelligent either. These Koreans like to write persuasively by telling about an issue in what used to seem, to me, a very mysterious fashion. They write about the issue, telling various points about it. Then, they write about it again, using some of those points, plus other factors to explain the issue. And, they might repeat this technique several times. In some ways their essays seem like Agatha Christie thrillers: They tease me with information but never really tell me "who done it" or, in the case of a persuasive writing assignment, what it is they wish to validate. As they progress through these essays, each repeat contains elements of what has come before, but new ideas are introduced. These students are arranging the data to help the reader think through the issues. The arrangement may lead an understanding reader to reach a kind of consensus of meaning by the end of the written piece. As items are introduced and eliminated, the reader must follow the various additions and subtractions, attempt to decipher the underlying logic, yet still infer the main idea. However, a typical American faculty member will rarely be sure of the central claim, but may obtain information about various aspects of the issue under discussion. Usually, such writing is not well rewarded by American faculty.

Or consider the case of some Native-American languages, many of which were oral languages without written lexicon or text until this century. Let's use Lakota as our example. Lakota persuasion can, like English or Japanese, be blunt when presented as an order. But, in a more involved attempt at explanation or persuasion, the Lakota speaker will tell stories, often four or more, that are somehow related to the topic at hand. The speaker confirms his or her proposition through the stories, which, though they may not even mention the speaker's major claim, are intended to help the listener understand the situation and come to the same conclusion as the speaker (J. W. Smith, personal communication, 1995). Unlike the Korean repetitive technique, this Native-American technique may include stories that, to a non-Sioux or non-Lakota speaker, do not seem related; but the native speaker will generally "get the point" and understand the message being conveyed. Most American college faculty may appreciate the stories, but may also label the student as one who has "missed the boat" in terms of meeting the expectations of a rhetorical writing assignment.

I have also had interesting experiences with native Spanish-speaking students whose linguistic reliance on passive reflexive verbs (e.g., instead of saying, "I dropped the watch on the floor," one can, in Spanish, say, "The watch dropped itself on the floor") has led them into what I call the "backdoor approach" to rhetoric. In English, they may use lots of passive voice, offer cautious description rather than a claim, and list facts to support that description rather than making critical connections between a thesis and the evidence, that is, telling *why* a claim is valid.

Other cultural and linguistic groups have different ways of approaching writing assignments, too. Consider the student who speaks Ebonics or Black Urban Dialect; I've had Ebonics-speaking students who write with such rhythm that they do not even need a drumbeat (also see Comfort, chap. 7, this volume). Some depend on the rhythm and repetition as a persuasive technique and are disappointed to find it doesn't work well in a history paper or in a presentation in sociology class, even though it might work well in a music or poetry class. Most academic writing depends on the arrangement of ideas, claims, and supporting factors so that the readers interact with the text and are informed or persuaded by it. Students must keep their audience clearly in mind and write for the expectations held by their readers or listeners.

Students who come from culture and language spheres that employ such varied native language rhetorical techniques often tell me that they feel as if their brains are being turned inside out when they have to state their main idea, or make a claim, or provide a strong thesis for the audience. They don't know how to think in English, they say. What does my professor mean by "stating a main point," they ask? Why do I have to tell you what I want you to know; don't you understand? What has perhaps not been given to these students in all their years of English training are essential components that enable them to present their ideas in a Western rhetorical arrangement of the type expected by the academy.

These students may have learned that subjects usually come before verbs in a sentence, but they often have not explored the relationship between the subject and the verb, nor the transactions that result from that relationship. They may fail to realize the logical connections between the ideas they are expressing; or, conversely, they understand the connections but may convey them in a home language structure that is unfamiliar and frequently not understood by their professors. Herein lies the dilemma: how to help these students master the academic form and function of English in order to write the descriptive and persuasive text required by our colleges and universities.

Leech (1987) defined two theories, stylistics and functionalism, that inform our discussion. Understanding these theories provides insight that will help us enable our multicultural students to link facts, ideas, and evidence to a claim in order to produce coherent, persuasive writing for academic purposes.

Stylistics is the study of writing style in order to explicate the relationship between the form of the text and its potential interpretation. In other words, does the writing style in which ideas are communicated enable the reader to understand the author's intent and meaning? *Functionalism* aims to explain not only those formal, internal properties such as agent–verb relations, but to also examine the contribution of language to larger systems such as culture, society, belief systems, and so forth (Leech, 1987, p. 76).

Thus, understanding the stylistic and functional properties of written text enables us to understand why what is said or written in a certain way is more or less effective in describing, analyzing, or persuading, or why certain text better conveys the notions of the author; we and our students can be critical readers. But, if the students' cultural and linguistic styles and functions do not match those expected in the academy, they may have difficulties.

Furthermore, since writing at the college level typically requires transactions between the writer and the reader, who are usually the student and the instructor or the student and other students, our students must determine which styles and which organizational patterns will best suit each transaction. Thus, the linguistic transactions that occur between writer and reader must take into account the underlying logical connections of ideas and evidence.

Typically, these transactions fit into Halliday's (1979) three levels of communication: interpersonal transaction, ideational transaction (one thing or idea represents another), or textual transaction (the text transfers the meaning, or conversely, the reader uses the text to construct meaning). The functional model coincides with a persuasive rhetorical position: In order to persuade, text must represent meaning and include interpersonal discourse that leads to ideational representation and understanding of the text. Linguists who adhere to functionalist ideals, such as Leech and Halliday, point out that if the writer (or speaker) has a functional orientation, in the end, the audience will gain meaning.

What does all of this mean on a practical basis for our students? If our students can visualize the connection between their relationship with the reader, the meaning they wish to represent, and the text as the delivery agent for the meaning, they can work toward clearly connecting their ideas and evidence when they write. But, how can they do this; how can they visualize the connection between ideas and readers, between text and ideas that lead the reader to agree with the student's point of view?

One quite simple method of introducing students to stylistically appropriate functional writing includes the recognition of logical sequencing. Perhaps native English speakers and majority–culture American students are able to "naturally" put their ideas in some sort of logical order, especially since they grew up with various kinds of ordered writing (narratives, laboratory instructions, schedules, etc.) that resemble the underlying structure of academic prose. But, as we have seen, many multicultural and multilingual students are familiar with different ways of ordering information: They tell multiple stories; they think and produce analysis by repeating and deleting to arrive at a conclusion through a kind of consensus; or they simply introduce discrete points and expect the listener or reader to come to the same conclusion they have.

In academic English, we use sequential patterns to organize and order information and to present it logically to our audience. Hauser (1986), in regard to spoken text but equally applicable to written text, stated that "rhetorical form presents a structured message, that structures have identifiable features, and that these features encourage relationships among speakers and listeners, and that structural patterns such as placement and association clusters provide an index to a speaker's motives" (p. 170). According to these structural patterns, native English speakers typically order facts, ideas, and every kind of information according to three categories: chronological ordering, psychological ordering (order for mental engagement), or rhetorical ordering (order for maximum persuasive effect). As readers, we construct meaning by making logical connections according to sequential ordering of information and relationships that are derived from inductive and deductive reasoning. We want to know what is most important and what is least important. And, in the academy, we depend on the author to inform us; if the author wants to persuade us, the text must be coherent and organized according to some sort of rhetorical structure.

Let's take a look at the effects of chronological ordering on ideas and text. In this simple example, the sentences are arranged chronologically:

Margarita woke up.
Margarita showered.
Margarita dressed.
Margarita ate breakfast.
Margarita went to school.
Margarita went to class.
Margarita studied hard.
The class ended.

In this instance, we have a description of Margarita's activities. We can make some assumptions about the time that these activities took place because we know that breakfast is a morning meal. But, every other activity in the list could take place at any time of the day or night; the information about breakfast is the point of relationship for all the other information.

In addition, we can see that, even though no transitions are used between the sentences, they are ordered in such a way that we recognize that some of the activities take place after others, as in going to school after eating breakfast, typical activities in American culture. They follow in a chronological sequence, and they are related through the reference to breakfast. Also, note that on another level these sentences, by themselves, demonstrate no coordination or subordination of activities except through the chronological sequencing.

Now, let's look at another example:

Margarita showered.
The class ended.
Margarita dressed.
Margarita went to class.
Margarita ate breakfast.
Margarita woke up.
Margarita went to class.
Margarita went to school.

In this instance, Margarita performs the same activities, but the sentences are not arranged chronologically; as a result, we have difficulty understanding the functional relationship of the text to the author's ideas. The function of the text itself is transactional and represents Margarita's actions, but we don't know the relationship of the actions. So, even though the text represents the activities Margarita performed, as ordered in the second example the sentences don't give us a clear idea of her morning behavior. The interpersonal transaction between the text and the reader is confusing because the logical chronological connection is missing.

Of course, we think our students should not have trouble organizing ideas and events chronologically. But they do. Students whose cultures use polychronic time, that is, nonlinear time, have difficulty ordering activities chronologically. Some languages do not overtly express the passage of time through their verbs; Vietnamese, for example, depends on a kind of auxiliary verb to express past and future. But, Vietnamese verbs themselves express a sort of habitual timing; as my students say, "Time is all around us; it doesn't come or go, it just is." English does express linearity through time; our verbs not only change form to fit various temporal periods, but they have added precision of locus in time through the use of auxiliaries. We view time as linear; it comes and it goes. But, a person speaking Vietnamese will "walk" today, "walk" yesterday, and "walk" tomorrow, too. Their auxiliaries signal past (and future), but not in the same way as we might move from simple present to past to past participle, and so forth. Thus, helping these students learn to order events chronologically, and to understand the sequencing of verbs, will help them make logical connections for their readers.

The second level of functional transactions, ideational or representative transactions, likewise poses problems for ESL students writing academic essays and research papers. When students wish to represent ideas, they frequently place the ideas in an order that does not make sense in English. There may be no coordination, subordination, or superordination of ideas or supporting factors. As we have seen, a student may present a list of discrete points and assume that the professor understands the conclusion or proposition the student wishes to claim. Other students may present ideas in stories or in consensus-building or -eliminating patterns that don't persuade an English-speaking audience to accept their ideas. Rhetoric is about informing and persuading, and academic prose uses a lot of rhetoric. Furthermore, the American academy expects certain structures; perhaps others ought to be accepted, but they usually are not. Thus, we need to help our students pick up a new trick, to shift their ideas into the academic rhetorical model in order to meet the expectations of their audience and successfully complete their course of study.

Thus, our students will benefit from a focus on mental engagement, from learning to handle psychological ordering. The audience will construct meaning based on the emphasis that students put on various elements of their text. Introducing elements of surprise, placing a demand on the reader to pay attention to details, or helping the reader reconstruct the author's intent are all necessary. If their text informs, tells the truth, is relevant, and is clearly written, students will engage their readers. Psychological ordering not only helps students fulfill the function of providing interaction and representation of ideas, but it also connects ideas logically and makes the text meaningful.

In this example about Tuan, let's observe the psychological impact of the statements:

Tuan went for a walk in the woods.
There he saw an animal.
The animal was bigger than Tuan.
The animal was a mountain lion.
Tuan was afraid of the lion.

In this case, the first two sentences are ordered chronologically, and the reader recognized "there" as subordinating the seeing of the animal to going for a walk. The next two sentences are not necessarily in chronological order, and the fifth sentence, because it follows the identification of the animal as a lion and depends on the common perception of wild lions as dangerous, provides a conclusion. Psychologically, we can easily connect the idea that Tuan went for a walk in the forest with seeing an animal. In the third sentence we learn that the animal is bigger than Tuan is. Well, lots of animals are bigger than Tuan, but this point seems interesting, and it is connected to the two previous sentences through the ideas that are later presented. So far, we have met Tuan, the forest, and an animal that's bigger than Tuan. The fourth sentence tells us why the size may be relevant, as it says the animal was a mountain lion. Well, that is startling news. We have had no hint of danger until this point. So, our author has introduced an element of surprise, which demands reader attention, that is, psychological engagement. Then, we learn that Tuan was afraid of the lion, which is natural. This set of sentences is ordered by psychological engagement; the sentences depend on each other for sequential information, not in a chronological fashion, but in a mental one.

Now, let's take a look at the same sentences in a different order. The psychological impact is not the same, and the logical connections the reader needs to make when reading the text are not provided.

The animal was bigger than Tuan.
Tuan went for a walk in the woods.
Tuan was afraid of the lion.
The animal was a mountain lion.
There he saw an animal.

In this set of sentences, we read the same information, but the logical progression is not present. Furthermore, a quick look at the articles *an* and *the* gives us a clue that something is awry. We know that the first time an idea is presented during discourse, the idea is indefinite; we use *a* or *an* to modify it. But, the second time the idea makes an appearance, it is a known entity, and we identify it as a definite idea with *the*. Notice the first, third, fourth, and fifth sentences. Where is the *an*—the indefinite animal/lion? In the fifth sentence, we have an indefinite animal after we have already defined the definite presence of a lion. The way we think of the information in the first set of sentences is logical; the presentation is functional because the reader can make an interpersonal transaction of understanding with the author, because the ideas are represented clearly, and because the text interacts psychologically with the reader to enable construction of meaning. In the second, unordered, set of sentences, the functionality is very weak. To understand the story in any kind of logical sense would require a guessing game; university faculty don't enjoy such games. They want their students to present information to which they can logically connect, information that clearly presents ideas so the reader does not have to try to decipher the meaning.

Rhetorical ordering is the third functional level of communication. Since rhetoric is persuasive, and because our students frequently need to write persuasively in their university classes, an understanding of rhetorical sequencing will be very useful. We have seen that some students do not naturally relate to linear time and thus have difficulty putting ideas in chronological sequence or understanding the various tenses and moods of English verbs. We have also seen that some students use circular or consensus-type discourse patterns to explain their ideas. While those techniques may work well in their home cultures or home languages, they typically confuse the native English speaker. Ordering ideas and hard evidence for maximum persuasive effect can be a difficult skill for these students to learn, and, again, the order depends on the purpose and on the audience: Does a text become more persuasive if the strongest evidence is presented first or last? When should a sentence begin with startling evidence or end with it? These are questions to be solved through rhetorical ordering for maximum persuasion.

One of the ways we can determine that rhetorical order is through critical thinking. Those of us who are native English speakers sometimes have "bright ideas" that "come to us out of the blue." More often, however, we think about a situation or problem and then arrive at a solution through careful sorting and ordering of related information. We may use a consensus framework of adding and eliminating factors, filtering information until we reach a conclusion, but most often we use two thinking patterns to do this: induction and deduction.

Induction is a pattern of thinking whereby we observe many specific instances of an action or we test many objects. After we have seen enough examples that we feel confident that any other similar instance would be the same as what we have seen, we induce a rule about those items. For example, let's say I buy a pair of size 8 tennis shoes of a certain brand, and they fit very well. They wear well, but when they finally do wear out, I buy a second pair of the same brand shoes, same size, and they also fit well and wear well. Let's say I repeat this process again: same shoes, same size, same fit and wearability. By now, I can make some general "rules" for myself about those shoes: Size 8 fits well, the shoes wear well. I have induced a rule about the shoes, and the process I have gone through is called induction.

Now that I have the rule, I can go to the shoe store and look at a pair of those tennis shoes and say, "Oh, those shoes fit well and wear well, too," without ever trying them on or wearing them. I have a rule about the shoes, and I can deduce that other shoes of the same brand and size will fit my rule. This process of making a judgment about a specific case based on a general rule is known as *deduction*.

Teaching multilingual and multicultural students how to induce and deduce consciously does them a great favor. They can learn to make judgments based on evidence, and they will understand the relationships of the individual case to the general rule. These relationships will also help students predict how their language choices will affect their readers. If students make comments "out of the blue" and aside from the context that induction and deduction provide, those comments may not convey the intended meaning. When students write arguments, and they want to write to persuade, they need to support their claims using induction and deduction. If they're writing any kind of persuasive text, induction and deduction will help them convey clear connections between the evidence and their conclusion about the topic.

In addition to the relationships between evidence and rules or between evidence and conclusions, we want to consider the interrelationships brought about by coordination or subordination of ideas. As we have seen in storytelling languages, in some cases telling several stories with the same level of importance enables the speaker to convey meaning. And, in languages that persuade by pointing out discrete points, those points are often presented at the same level of importance. We might say that the ideas coordinate; they work together on the same level to convey meaning. More likely, however, an American instructor will view the ideas as items on a list. However, the ideas could be ordered chronologically or psychologically to provide rhetorical meaning. Here, however, we are concerned with the importance of the ideas; if they are coordinated, they may or may not offer mutual support. If subordinated or superordinated, the ideas will present levels of priority or importance.

For example, we might write: "President Thomas Jefferson encouraged development of fruit crops. President Dwight Eisenhower encouraged the development of fruit crops. Two presidents encouraged development of fruit crops." In these sentences, we do not know whether Eisenhower encouraged fruit crops as a result of Jefferson's earlier efforts. There is no logical subordination of ideas except with the third sentence, which could stand alone but, if presented with the two preceding sentences, psychologically depends on the information for meaning. However, the ideas themselves are coordinated rather than subordinated; there is no priority or established importance.

For an example of a subordinated idea set, we can look at nearly any sentence with a dependent clause subordinated to the main clause in the sentence. In the example "President Nixon, who was the President more than 6 years ago, resigned because he committed a crime," we have subordinate information, "because he committed a crime," that gives meaning to the main idea of the sentence: President Nixon resigned. The subordinate information explains *why* he resigned, and it provides psychological and chronological information to the reader. Also, the relative clause "who was the President more than 6 years ago" is subordinate to the main notion of Nixon resigning. That subordinate information provides background information to the reader, but it is not necessary to the agent–verb relationship in "President Nixon . . . resigned."

Finally, we find that coherence is a major factor in persuasive writing. If a student orders information chronologically, psychologically, and rhetorically, the information will at least be presented in a logical order with a connecting factor of time, mental engagement, or maximum persuasive effect. Even so, however, students will produce smoother text flow if they make good use of transitions, which have the effect of giving the reader a bridge between various points. In the sentences about Margarita and Tuan, we have no transitions, but let's take a look at the examples that follow; notice the smoother connection between ideas when transitions and connecting words are in place.

> At 6 o'clock in the morning, Margarita woke up. After crawling out of bed, she showered and dressed. Then she ate breakfast and went to school. Once inside the building, Margarita went to class where she studied hard. Finally the class ended.

In the paragraph about Margarita, we have added a definite time, plus the words *after, then, and, once inside the building, where*, and *finally*. These terms not only bridge the facts mentioned, but they further contribute toward the chronological ordering, and thus to the functional connection of ideas in a logical sequence.

> One day, Tuan went for a walk in the woods, and there he saw an animal, which was bigger than he was. Then he noticed that the animal was a lion, and he became afraid.

In the paragraph about Tuan and the lion, we also have new terms: *one day, and there, which, then, that*, and *and*. These words have the same bridging function, and they contribute not only to the chronology but also to the psychological ordering of ideas by building coherency.

Another exercise that is useful in helping students produce functional prose that contains logical connections employs the use of syllogisms with well-ordered premises. We have probably all learned basic logic, but here are three examples of logical syllogisms. In each case, two premises that are related but not subordinate are presented as evidence for the validity of the conclusion. In the first example, A = B, B = C, A = C, there is no question of the validity as the factors are equal. But, in the second example, Some A = B, Some B = C, Some A = C, we have a semantic interchange that could affect the truth of the conclusion. If Some A in the first premise is the same Some A as in the conclusion, then the conclusion is valid. But, as we know, the word *some* is variable; we don't quite know how much or what *some* is, and the writer would need to define the term in order to provide clarification.

The third syllogism is a bit more complex:

> College students are not bald.
> He is bald.
> Therefore he is not a college student.

This syllogism contains two premises: "College students are not bald" and "He is bald." But, to then conclude that he must not be a college student could be valid or not depending on whether we assume the first premise is valid in all cases. In real life, some college students are bald, so the first premise falls on account of faulty basis. In this case, the premise is false, and the syllogism is also false. However, keep in mind that even with a faulty premise or a faulty relationship between premises, the conclusion could be valid in some cases if the conclusion can stand alone. For example:

> Dogs are carnivores.
> Dogs eat fish.
> Therefore, humans are carnivores.

In this case, the conclusion is valid apart from the premises but not in conjunction with them. Syllogisms make use of coordination and subordination; they also utilize psychological ordering and may involve chronological ordering as well. Using syllogisms to teach logical and psychological ordering is a useful exercise, one that can be applied to the logic and structure of longer text.

As a final example of ordering for rhetorical purposes, let's examine the first paragraph and the supporting points Tuchman (1989), a well-known historian, used in her critique of the Presidency. She wrote:

> Owing to the steady accretion of power in the executive over the last forty years, the institution of the Presidency is not now functioning as the constitution intended, and this malfunction has become perilous to the state. What needs to be abolished, or fundamentally modified, I believe, is not the executive power as such, but the executive power as exercised by a single individual. (p. 273)

It is clear that Tuchman argues, as she proposes her central claim, that the single-individual Presidency should be abolished. Notice that she precedes her thesis with an introductory statement that gives the reader an occasion for reading and understanding her argument. As her essay evolves, she supports her argument with the following points:

1. . . . the office has become too complex for one . . .
2. . . . the Chief . . . form(s) policy as a reflection of his personality and ego . . .
3. . . . the President is subject to no advisers who hold office independently of him . . .
4. . . . Cabinet government is a perfectly feasible operation . . . (pp. 273–274).

Tuchman's (1989) evidence is not presented in a chronological order; in fact, the evidence is presented as coordinate points—each carries equal weight.

She does, however, use psychological ordering as she begins with the President as "one" and moves from the complexity of office through character, assistants, and finally to a Cabinet government. Her information is ordered rhetorically as well: She aims for maximum persuasive power by moving from the individual (specific) to a body able to govern (general), the Cabinet. The full text of her argument contains related details psychologically and rhetorically ordered to interact with her readers to develop a strong body of support for her thesis. They are able to connect her evidence logically to her meaning. Her text reaches the reader through interpersonal transaction (she voices her personal opinion), ideational transaction (she proposes an argument and supports it), and textual transaction (her ideas are ordered psychologically and rhetorically for her reader). Her text is functional; her readers are able to construct the meaning she intends to convey.

Using Leech's (1987) notions of functional language, which involve interpersonal transactions between the writer or speaker and the audience, ideational transactions that represent the concerns and beliefs of the writer, and textual transactions that present the ideas and the connections between what is written and the meaning derived or constructed by the reader, we have briefly touched on some means of enabling our multicultural and multilingual students to make logical connections in their university writing assignments. If students then learn to arrange and sequence their ideas and support by using chronological, psychological, and rhetorical structures, their compositions and presentations will be more readily understood and persuasive. Making logical connections in university writing can be problematic for multicultural and multilingual students, but with careful instruction and plenty of practice, students can learn to understand and purposefully make the transition from the logic and rhetorical structures of their home languages and cultures to those of academic English and culture, and back again. Our students certainly do not need to give up what works well in their home cultures and home languages, but we can give them new skills and ways of thinking to use in their persuasive writing in our classes and in their other courses.

REFERENCES

Halliday, M. A. K. (1979). Modes of meaning and modes of expression: Types of grammatical structure, and their determination by different semantic functions. In D. Allerton, E. Carney, & D. Holdroft (Eds.), *Function and context in linguistic analysis* (pp. 57–79). Cambridge, England: Cambridge University Press.

Hauser, G. A. (1986). *Introduction to rhetorical theory.* Prospect Heights, IL: Waveland Press.

Kaplan, R. B. (1972). *The anatomy of rhetoric: Prolegomena to a functional theory of rhetoric.* Philadelphia: The Center for Curriculum Development.

Kaplan, R. B. (1987). *Writing across languages: Analysis of L2 written text.* Reading, MA: Addison-Wesley.

Kennedy, G. A. (1998). *Comparative rhetoric: An historical and cross-cultural introduction.* New York: Oxford University Press.

Leech, G. (1987). Stylistics and functionalism. In N. Fabb et al. (Eds.), *The linguistics of writing* (pp. 76–88). New York: Methuen.

Purves, A. C., & Purves, W. C. (1986). Viewpoints: Cultures, text models, and the activity of writing. *Research in the Teaching of English, 12,* 107–118.

Tuchman, B. (1989). Should we abolish the presidency? In S. D. Spurgin (Ed.), *The power to persuade* (pp. 273–274). Englewood Cliffs, NJ: Prentice-Hall.

3

Contrastive Rhetoric and Resistance to Writing

Jan Corbett
Delaware Valley College

> *The word in language is half someone else's. It becomes "one's own" only when the speaker populates it with his own intention, his own accent.*
> —M. M. Bakhtin (1981, p. 293)

Although research in contrastive rhetoric has been successfully applied to the prescriptive writing pedagogy it was originally designed to support, compositionists have found it less relevant to contemporary pedagogies that focus on the social construction of knowledge.[1] Kaplan (1988) suggested a new research paradigm that responds to this problem by focusing on the sociolinguistic functions of texts. However, many researchers continue to apply studies with this broader focus to a prescriptive pedagogy, rather than using them to address the concerns of the contemporary writing classroom.[2] Leki (1997) argued that this is appropriate for second-language (L2) students because they are not interested in maintaining the differences they bring from their own languages, as social constructionists urge them to do (p. 242). She concluded that these students should be taught to "reproduce English norms" without being concerned about maintaining the rhetoric of their first language or about the "colonizing effects" of reproducing the rhetoric of the English language (p. 244).

I have come to believe, however, that the effort, and even trauma, associated with avoiding the rhetoric of a first language or with ignoring the "colo-

---

[1]See Leki (1991).

[2]Connor (1997) suggested that these studies can explain "why and how teachers should teach the expectations of the English-speaking audience to ESL writers," and help ESL students "feel good about themselves knowing that their writing in English is not bad simply because it exhibits some rhetorical features of their first language" (p. 208).

31

nizing effects" of writing in the English language causes some students to be blocked in their writing or to exhibit other forms of resistance. In this chapter, I suggest that these students are unable to negotiate conflicting rhetorics because they contain conflicting ideologies, and students do not have the means of writing about these ideologies without being rhetorically entangled in their contradictions. A pedagogy which acknowledges this conflict will enable L2 students, as well as students whose first language is English but whose rhetoric represents diverse economic and social cultures, to use their resistance as a heuristic by helping them understand it as a rhetorical problem that calls for a rhetorical solution. One such solution is for students to create a new discourse that allows them to negotiate the borders between conflicting rhetorics.

RHETORICAL CONFLICT

Studies in contrastive rhetoric have acknowledged rhetorical conflict, but this conflict has not always been viewed as a barrier to acquiring skill in writing in a different language or discourse. Kaplan's (1966) early "doodles" graphically illustrate the competing thought patterns of different cultures, but he subsumes the potential conflict between these patterns into a formalist concern with imitating the thought patterns of English, a theoretical approach he has since questioned (Kaplan, 1988, p. 278). However, even in his later work, Kaplan seems to suggest that rhetorical conflict relating to writer/reader responsibility, audience, and the purpose of writing can be contained in a pedagogy that enables the student to "manage" the conventions related to writing in English (Kaplan, 1988, p. 296).

Other studies illustrate the difficulty students have in managing these conventions. Matalene's (1985) account of teaching college English in Shanxi Province in China illustrates the very real conflict students experience in moving from the rhetoric of one language to another, and the way their resistance to this transition interferes with writing in English. When Matelene asked her students to keep personal journals of their attempts to learn English, she discovered that they were not familiar with expressive journal writing and did not feel comfortable doing it. As the semester progressed, the number of journals turned in "gradually and silently diminished" (p. 791) and Matalene concluded that the rhetoric of post-Romantic Westerners, which values originality, individuality, and what we call the "authentic voice," cannot be co-opted by Chinese students for ideological reasons; they are expected to imitate the ideas and style of respected writers. Matalene's experience illustrates the effect of competing (not just contrasting) rhetorics, and it foregrounds the ideological basis of rhetorical conflict in second-language acquisition.

Lu's (1987) personal account of her struggle to negotiate between writing in English and Chinese provides additional insight into rhetorical conflict. Lu grew up in China, but because her parents wanted her to attend Cambridge, she spoke English at home while attending a Chinese day school. During the Maoist revolution, Lu was forced to write Chinese essays in a working-class formula by imitating sample essays. She described her experience of moving between the two languages as one of self-doubt, alienation, and eventually silence:

> The homogeneity of home and of school implied that only one discourse could and should be relevant in each place. It led me to believe I should leave behind, turn a deaf ear to, or forget the discourse of the other when I crossed the boundary dividing them. I expected myself to set down one discourse whenever I took up another just as I would take off or put on a particular set of clothes for school or home. . . . (However), having to speak aloud in the voice I had just silenced each time I crossed the boundary kept both voices active in my mind. . . . I could not use the interaction comfortably and constructively. Both my parents and my teachers had implied that my job was to prevent that interaction from happening. My sense of having failed to accomplish what they had taught silenced me. (pp. 445–446)

Lu was able to overcome her silence only when she was physically removed from her rhetorical situation and, as a mature adult, was able to see writing as a dialectical process in which she was constantly repositioning herself. Although she feels that she ultimately benefited from her experience with two languages, the vivid description of her earlier trauma provides a compelling illustration of the pain students experience as they try to negotiate conflicting rhetorics.

In our own classrooms, we often see this pain expressed as resistance to writing, a kind of writer's block that resembles the silence both Matalene and Lu observed. Donny (whose real name is Dong, but who prefers the Americanization of his Vietnamese name) provides an interesting example of this resistance. He came to my office to discuss his inability to respond to an assignment that required him to compare two essays about living in two cultures, or to compare his own experience to that described in one of the essays.

Donny had chosen to write about his own experience in living in two cultures, but he was unable to write a single sentence on the topic. He was obviously agitated as he discussed his problem, but each suggestion that he explore the subject in more depth met with only halfhearted attempts. "I can't think of anything," he said over and over, with what I finally realized was not a lack of affect, but very strong resistance. In desperation, I asked, "What do you *not* want to write?" This question seemed to provide an opening for Donny to explain the difficulty he had experienced in living in two worlds: His parents had brought him to the United States when he was 3 years old, and he quickly learned to speak English. But he was sent back to Vietnam to live with his grandparents during his high school years so that he could identify with his

Vietnamese culture. He had now returned to the United States to attend college, and he felt that he did not belong in either country. Donny articulated—perhaps for the first time—his difficulty in deciding which culture he valued most. While attending public school in the United States, he had been taught to value American culture. But when he returned to Vietnam, he was persuaded that his first allegiance was to the country of his ancestors, a country which viewed the war his parents escaped as "the American war."

He described his feelings as a kind of retreat into nothingness. "I just kind of go blank," he said. There seemed to be nothing there, even when he was prodded to produce a simple free-writing exercise. This nothingness resembles the writer's block Nin (1969) described as being "mysteriously exhausted, deep down" (p. 85) and Woolf (1954) described as having a brain that is "as blank as a window" (p. 121). Although some theorists view this blockage as an early stage in the writing process (Kubasak, 1988), or as based in cognitive (Rose, 1985) or emotional (Bergler, 1950) problems, I came to believe that Donny's blockage represented an inability to negotiate two competing rhetorics because these rhetorics represented conflicting ideologies: the communal ideology of Vietnam, in which individual voice is sublimated to the will of the community, and the self-actualizing ideology of the United States, with its rhetoric of individual autonomy and authority. Writing about living in Vietnam meant engaging the rhetoric/ideology of that culture, and writing about living in the United States meant making entirely different rhetorical and ideological choices. Donny was entangled in conflicting rhetorics and ideologies and, like Matalene's students and Lu, he was silenced.

RHETORIC AND IDEOLOGY

Although some studies in contrastive rhetoric have pointed to the imbrication of rhetoric and ideology, their pedagogical implications have not always been viewed as relevant to the goals of contrastive rhetoric research, as pointed out in the introduction to this chapter. To understand these implications, we need to turn to Bakhtin, whose writings focus on language but, according to Stewart (1983), contest many of the conclusions of a formalist study of linguistics.

Stewart (1983) pointed out that, although Bakhtin wrote out of a linguistic tradition, he might more appropriately be labeled a theorist of ideology than a theorist of linguistics, because he inverted the premises of traditional linguistic theory in order to show the unsystematic, conflicted nature of writing and speaking (p. 266) and the basis for this conflict in the relationship between language and ideology (p. 273). Bakhtin claimed that languages, and the rhetorical conventions in which each language functions, are always ideological. In *The Dialogic Imagination* (Bakhtin, 1981), for example, he described languages as "specific points of view on the world, forms for conceptualizing the world in words, specific world views" which live a "real life" (pp.

291–292). As a "living, socio-ideological concrete thing" (p
becomes one's own when it is appropriated and adapted to i.
tions:

> Prior to this moment of appropriation the word does not exist in ._ .ceutral and impersonal language (it is not, after all, out of a dictionary that the speaker gets his words!) but rather it exists in other people's mouths, in other people's contexts, serving other people's intentions: it is from there that one must take the word, and make it one's own. (pp. 293–294)

Learning to use a language thus becomes a process of acquiring and adapting ideas. In an introduction to his theory of literary scholarship, Bakhtin (Bakhtin/Medvedev, 1978)[3] described the environment in which this acquisition takes place:

> Social man is surrounded by ideological phenomena, by objects-signs (*veshch'-znak*) of various types and categories: by words in the multifarious forms of their realization (sounds, writing, and the others), by scientific statements, religious symbols and beliefs, works of art, and so on. All of these things in their totality comprise the ideological environment which forms a solid ring around man. (p. 14)

The rhetorical conventions that are learned in this environment shape our individual consciousness; in fact, Bakhtin (Bakhtin/Medvedev, 1978) claimed that our consciousness "can only become a consciousness by being realized in the forms of the ideological environment . . . in language, in conventionalized gesture, in artistic image, in myth, and so on" (p. 14).

But these forms, and the ideologies they represent, are always changing, because, as Bakhtin (Bakhtin/Medvedev, 1978) pointed out, "contradictions are always present, constantly being overcome and reborn" (p. 14). Thus, the ideological environment is constantly in an "active dialectical process of generation" (p. 14), a process that Bakhtin (1981) called "dialogized heteroglossia" when he described it in relation to the novel (p. 272).

This heteroglossia is often ignored. Bakhtin's (1981) example is a peasant who is unaware that he lives in several languages: the languages of the church, his country, his family, and his local government. When he recognizes that these are not only different languages but that the ideological systems "that were indissolubly connected with these languages" contradicted each other and "in no way could live in peace and quiet with one another," he is faced with not only choosing among languages, but choosing among ideologies (p. 296).

---

[3]The text is generally attributed to Bakhtin, but Albert J. Wehrle argues in a preface to his translation that it was produced with the assistance or even collaboration of P. N. Medvedev. Thus, Wehrle explains that "the slash separating the names on the title page of (the) translation may be taken as the conventional signifier/signified bar" (p. xi).

Some theorists have misappropriated Bakhtin's (1981) concept of dialogized heteroglossia to suggest that a logical choice among ideologies can be made in a polite discussion where competing ideologies are equally respected and rationally discussed, a classroom which is uncontaminated by issues of authority or power. Giroux (1981) compared this ideal to the "undistorted communication" described by Habermas that he believed represented a context where "there is no room for manipulation, cultural invasion, conquest, and domination" (p. 139). In the real world, however, communication contexts are always contaminated, because the rhetoric in which ideas are communicated is shaped by the political forces and social practices that Foucault (1977) identified in his analysis of "discursive practices" (pp. 199–200). Conflicting rhetorics thus compete for dominance within the most polite dialogue, and this competition undermines the communication process. A similar conflict within individual writers can sometimes immobilize them, undermining their ability to write.

RESISTANCE TO COMPETING RHETORICS

The struggle for dominance between competing rhetorics is of special concern to compositionists who believe the writing classroom should represent a democratic ideal in which differences are not only tolerated but valued, and where power is shared equally among all students. Berlin (1991) described one attempt to reproduce this ideal in a writing course that combined the methods of semiotic analysis with social-epistemic rhetoric.[4] Berlin's teaching assistants were asked to problematize students' experiences related to such cultural practices as advertising, work, play, education, gender, and individuality so that they would challenge the ideological codes they brought to college. Many students resisted this goal, however, and Berlin concluded that students "find it difficult—even painful—to offer any critique of the set of cultural codes they daily enact" (p. 52). Although Berlin saw this resistance as evidence of a kind of cultural bondage in which the students were "victims of political strategies that have held their generation personally responsible for the failures of economic and social policies over which they have had no control" (p. 53), I think it also represents an inability to move out of the rhetorical context in which their ideology has been acquired because they have no rhetorical means of escaping this ideology, no alternative language that embodies the more "humane and socially equitable economic and political arrangements" (p. 50) valued in the course design. When the students "described advertisements as blatantly sexist, class-biased, and patently dishonest" and then "went on to

---

[4]Berlin (1998) defined social-epistemic rhetoric as committed to democratic practices, that is, "practices that work for the equitable distribution of the power to speak and write among all groups in a society" (p. 408).

praise them for their success in selling a product" (p. 52), they were reflecting the values of the capitalistic culture in which they had learned the word "advertising." They did not have a noncapitalistic language that would allow them to critique these values.

France and Fitts (1994) described a similar kind of resistance to ideological transformation in a classroom in which they asked students to analyze "social inequities" in practices related to gender, the media, and rock culture (p. 53). Although students were able to analyze these practices and to recognize unequal power relations, they often invented rather subtle ways to resist their own conclusions, inventing rhetorical strategies to "reconcile their findings to the ideology . . . that the assignments were calculated to problematize" (p. 54). Like Berlin's students, these students were unable to use their native rhetoric to critique the ideology embedded in this rhetoric, and they continued to be dominated by this ideology.

Resisting a dominant ideology is even more difficult for English-as-a-second-language (ESL) students and for students who do not see themselves as participating socially or economically in a dominant culture. These students are asked to critique an ideology in a language they have not yet mastered, and whose mastery implicates them in the ideology they are being asked to critique. I think this explains the resistance that students like Donny/Dong experience, as well as the resistance Fox (1990) described among basic writers who avoid acquiring the academic discourse of the White majority culture because their identity has developed in opposition to this culture and they do not want to join the "opposition" (p. 74). (See also Comfort, chap. 7, this volume.)

Rhetorical conflict can lead to resistance to writing whether it is encountered in a homogeneous classroom, an ESL classroom, or a multicultural classroom. Because contrastive rhetoric research has often marginalized this conflict, I have found it useful to classify the forms in which I have personally confronted it in writing classes, as a way of examining the way it disrupts writing. The following cases illustrate this taxonomy.

REPRESSED CONFLICTS

In the first case, students are involved in collaborative writing projects that are threatened by rhetorical conflict that is repressed; it is so traumatic that it operates at a subconscious level to undermine their ability to fully engage in a writing task.

The context is a business communication class composed of students from a variety of cultures who have organized into self-selected writing groups. Each group is identifying communication problems within their university, residence, or employment community and preparing both oral and written reports which recommend ways to eliminate these barriers. In an early stage of the project, the class has been invited to vote on "funding" each project, based on the clarity of the problem statement and the appropriateness of the research design.

There are five projects and four have been "funded." The final group is composed of three African-American women who plan to research the communication breakdown between welfare recipients and the state legislators who are considering denying welfare to any client who has an additional child after she has been approved for assistance. Not realizing that two of the women are mothers receiving welfare, some students begin to discuss the issue rather than the group's proposed research, asking whether people have children "just so they can stay on welfare" and why "our hard-earned money" should go to "support women who just stay home and have more kids." When a vote on funding is taken, several students deny it.

The African-American group is immobilized by this rejection. They decide to change their topic, but when they are unable to find research to support a new topic, the two members who are on welfare outvote the third member in a decision to return to their original subject. These two later come to my office to complain that the third member has not been attending their meetings.

Meanwhile, remnants of the class discussion are cropping up in the work of other groups. The chair of a group that is researching communication in a high school sex education course stops me after class to ask whether her group should use a statistic they have uncovered: that African Americans have a higher percentage of teen pregnancies than any other group. She is concerned "because"—she glances around—"you know. . . ." She does not finish the sentence. A group working on campus vandalism asks me about a paragraph on which they cannot agree; it attributes much of the vandalism to the African-American residents of the community surrounding the university. Finally, a group researching the glass ceiling at a nearby DuPont office gives an interim report on their project and the student who initially challenged the welfare project is emboldened to refute the need for affirmative action; subsequently, four males in the DuPont group miss meetings and writing deadlines, forcing the one woman in the group to complete the final report.

On reflection, it appears that a subtext is emerging around the issues of race, class, and gender that were introduced by the African-American group. Like a computer virus, this subtext is attacking the capacity of all the groups to produce coherent texts because it is unacknowledged and repressed—in the unfinished sentence of the sex education group chair and the physical withdrawal of the four men in the glass ceiling group, as well as the withdrawal of the nonwelfare student from the African-American group.

The subtext is repressed because the class is unable to deal with ideological and rhetorical conflict. The original discussion caught them by surprise, bringing to the surface conflicting ideologies that were embedded in conflicting rhetorics. The student who initially objected to the welfare topic expressed a classist and racist ideology in rhetoric that diminished and marginalized the

African-American women, with phrases like "our hard-earned money" and women who "just stay home and have more kids." At the same time, the group working on welfare introduced values that were quite different in a rhetoric that was unfamiliar to many students. Because the class did not know how to handle the conflict between these rhetorics and ideologies, they repressed it. But the conflict did not disappear; it operated like a repressed trauma to undermine the writing of all the groups.

SUPPRESSED CONFLICT

Rhetorical conflict is not always repressed; sometimes it is acknowledged but intentionally suppressed to avoid the embarrassment of expressing an opinion that might be interpreted as biased. Because suppressed conflict is initially hidden, we sometimes fail to recognize it or to acknowledge its effect on writing, as the following case illustrates.

Charles is a Caucasian junior who is retaking composition in order to improve his grade point average. He is a good writer and offers helpful advice to his writing group, especially to the two Japanese members, Ayako and Shuichi. He becomes almost a mentor to these students, and his conversations with them extend beyond the class period.

In a conference on his research paper topic, Charles shares his interest in Japanese culture and his goal of seeking employment in Japan after graduation. He has chosen to write about differences in the Japanese and American systems of education, but he is unable to decide on a thesis. When pushed to explain why he is interested in this aspect of Japanese culture, he simply reviews his interest in Japan. Then, with increasing agitation, he explains that it is unfair to compare American students' achievements with those of Japanese students, since many Japanese parents pay for their children to receive extensive tutoring outside the classroom. He seems to be leaning toward a thesis that would argue that the American educational system should not be criticized from the standpoint of the success of the Japanese system, thus taking a kind of defensive, nationalistic approach to the issue. But after writing this thesis statement out, he fails to share it with his writing group.

Charles misses the deadline for an initial draft of his paper, and says that he is having trouble writing it. This is surprising, because he has written his other essays with a great deal of confidence and submitted them on time. But the reason becomes clear in a later conversation in which Charles reveals his rhetorical dilemma: As he began to write a nationalistic defense of the American system of education, he became entangled in a nationalistic rhetoric which he realizes would be offensive to his Japanese colleagues. Because this rhetoric is the only way he can express his beliefs, he gives up his thesis, but he is having difficulty finding another, more acceptable argument. He has consciously suppressed his original thesis in order to avoid overt conflict, but the energy required to maintain this suppression—and to find a rhetorical means of spanning the two cultures—drains him of the energy he needs to develop a new argument.

OVERT CONFLICT

Although I failed to initially recognize Charles' suppressed conflict or the repressed conflict in the business communications class, there is another kind of rhetorical conflict that is immediately evident: overt conflict. As a humanist professor, I experience the most personal trauma when this kind of conflict emerges. Students are also traumatized by overt conflict, as the following experience with a composition class illustrates.

It is nearly the end of the semester, and students are giving 5-minute synopses of their research papers on topics related to multiculturalism. Much like the students described by France and Fitts (1994), these students have found unique rhetorical strategies to subvert the rhetoric of tolerance advocated by their multicultural reader. Dan argues that every immigrant should learn English, as he had to do when he moved to the United States from Germany in the fourth grade. Jack claims that "political correctness" represents a new form of censorship. Irene, a first-generation immigrant from Greece, questions why Native Americans were treated as savages by European settlers.

There are no African Americans in the class, so when Max, a Caucasian student from a blue-collar neighborhood in South Philadelphia, describes his paper on the history of the Ku Klux Klan, the students respond with a polite series of questions about his research. Then Abigail, an articulate student who has supported tolerance on a variety of multicultural issues, asks, "Why did you write about the Ku Klux Klan? Don't you know what they did to Blacks?"

"Sure," Max replies. "I hate them niggers. I'd join the Klan, myself, if I could." He then describes growing up in a neighborhood where he was constantly drawn into a conflict over whether Whites or Blacks owned the public basketball court. "You go through their neighborhood, they jump you," he says. "They go through our neighborhood, we do the same thing. They hate us as much as we hate them."

There is a stunned silence in the room. Then Abigail says, "My brother was shot by one of them, but I don't hate 'em." This seems to end the discussion; no one wants to support either Abigail or Max. The introduction of a rhetoric of hate into a classroom that has focused on tolerance has traumatized the class, and they do not have the rhetorical means to respond to this trauma.

My reflection on this experience brings the realization that Max is not the only student who has opposed the values of tolerance and cooperation that have been foregrounded in the class. Many students have found these values, and the rhetoric in which they have been expressed, to be quite different from their own experiences. They have repressed this dissonance in class discussions, but they have been emboldened to express it in their research papers because they have found support for their racist or nationalist opinions in academic sources. By incorporating quotations from these sources into their essays, they believe they have produced academic discourse; in reality, they have reproduced the rhetoric in which their original ideologies were formulated.

Jack, the student who writes about political correctness, for example, supports his resistance to multiculturalism with what appears to be a legitimate source: "According to Carol Iannone, a teacher at NYU, 'multiculturalists want to impart a knowledge of America's crimes, sins, and transgressions to young people'" (Di Salvatore, 1995, p. 4). Unfortunately, however, Jack has lifted this quote from its original context in order to maintain a rhetoric that is consistent with his own. This strategy enables him to overtly express his resistance to multiculturalism, but it also keeps him from acquiring the skills necessary to engage in an academic discourse that critiques sources and evaluates opposing viewpoints. Other students use a similar means of expressing their own ideology, but they are shocked into silence when confronted with Max's "street" rhetoric which, in effect, unmasks their own strategies of resistance.

These examples of repressed, suppressed, and overt rhetorical conflict illustrate the traumas students face when they attempt to write in rhetorical forms that contradict or marginalize the ideas embedded in their native rhetoric. If we recognize the potential for this resistance, and its basis in ideological conflict, we will understand why students are not always able to adopt the rhetorical forms of standard English or academic discourse. We need to find ways to help these students acknowledge that contrastive rhetorics are sometimes competing rhetorics, and to use this understanding to extricate themselves from the ideological entanglement this competition engenders.

RESPONDING TO RHETORICAL CONFLICT

Interestingly, some of the students in the preceding cases found their own unique ways to manage rhetorical conflict. In retrospect, their methods seem to exhibit an almost instinctual understanding of the need for developing new rhetorical forms that mediate conflicting rhetorics.

In the first case, the African-American writing group received permission to invite an articulate county welfare executive to present part of their oral report. She used a discourse that contained rhetorical forms borrowed from her own African-American heritage as well as forms with which the Caucasian students were familiar. This "bridge" discourse allowed her to express and contain the two competing rhetorics, while mediating their conflicting values. By extension, it provided both the African-American writing group and the Caucasian students with a rhetoric in which they could express, and even trans-form, their ideological conflict.

Charles, the student who suppressed his rhetorical conflict, also used a new discourse to escape his ideological entanglement. Instead of adopting the tra-ditional form of an academic essay, which would have required him to hierar-chicize the values of an American or Japanese education, he developed a hybrid form that allowed him to argue that the Japanese system is appropriate for the Japanese culture and the American system is appropriate for the Amer-ican culture. This approach enabled him to incorporate the values of both sys-tems in one paper and to appropriate the contrasting rhetorics in which these values are embedded without becoming traumatized by their conflicting ide-ologies.

Unfortunately, the students engaged in overt conflict did not reach a solu-tion that was as satisfactory as the solutions in the first two cases. They were silenced by a rhetoric of hate that they did not want to adopt but that many could not refute because they shared the ideology on which it was based. Since their trauma occurred at the end of the semester, it was not appropriately addressed. Instead of the students being changed by this experience, the pro-fessor was changed: I concluded that I needed to learn more about the ideolo-gy in which students' rhetorics are based before confronting them with the competing rhetorics of a multicultural reader, and to explore the imbrication of rhetoric and ideology. In many ways, this resolve led to the writing of this chapter.

I think it is interesting, however, that students in the first two cases instinc-tively developed a means of incorporating diverse rhetorical forms and their embedded ideologies into a new discourse. Their strategies bear some resem-blance to Bakhtin's (1981) description of a novelist reworking the heteroglos-sia of the novel:

> The prose writer as a novelist does not strip away the intentions of others from the heteroglot language of his works, he does not violate those socio-ideological cultural horizons . . . that open up behind heteroglot languages—rather, he wel-comes them into his work. The prose writer makes use of words that are already populated with the social intentions of others and compels them to serve his own new intentions, to serve a second master. (pp. 299–300)

The ability to make words one's own implies an ability to make ideas one's own and to create new rhetorical forms for the expression of these ideas. It is the creative act in which novelists engage, but it is not limited to writing a novel. Lu (1992) advocated a similar process when she suggested that composition-ists help students who are facing rhetorical conflict use that conflict to devel-op what Anzaldúa (1990) called a "mestiza consciousness" by developing "a tolerance for contradiction and ambivalence, learning to sustain contradiction and turn ambivalence into a new consciousness—a third element which is greater than the sum of its several parts" (quoted in Lu, 1992, p. 888).

This consciousness is different for every student, and the discourse in which it is expressed contains unique rhetorical forms, just as novels by different authors contain unique stylistics. But the mestizo quality of the discourse enables students to use it to negotiate the borders between conflicting rhetorics and to escape the ideological entanglement that causes resistance to writing. Anzaldúa (1990) explained the way this happens:

> [The new *mestiza*] can be jarred out of ambivalence by an intense, and often painful, emotional event which inverts or resolves the ambivalence. I'm not sure exactly how. The work takes place underground—subconsciously. It is work that the soul performs. That focal point or fulcrum, that juncture where the *mestiza* stands, is where phenomena tend to collide. It is where the possibility of uniting all that is separate occurs. (p. 379)

Because each student must find the unique focal point where "the soul performs" its work, a mestizo discourse cannot be taught; that is, students cannot learn to adopt its rhetorical conventions in the way they may be instructed to adopt the conventions of the English language. However, some composition-ists have developed a pedagogy that provides an environment in which this "soul work" takes place. One of their methods is to engage students in a form of contrastive rhetoric research that focuses on discourse analysis.

PEDAGOGICAL RESPONSES TO COMPETING RHETORICS

Compositionists who use discourse analysis to analyze problems in competing rhetorics go beyond the analysis of formal structures that is found in early con-trastive rhetoric research to analyze the ideological context of rhetorical forms. Spellmeyer (1989), for example, suggested that students should learn to analyze their own discourse from the perspective of a new, unfamiliar dis-course:

> Like the fieldworker in Jogjakarta, students unfamiliar with the discourse of, say, historical inquiry or political theory can never "go native," no matter how earnest-ly they try to silence their voices from the past, because this persistent murmur will become audible and coherent—will become a part of their conscious life—only after they have listened to other, unaccustomed voices. We can understand Javanese culture in terms of our culture, and we can understand ours within the problematic created by our encounter with the Javanese, but we cannot under-stand either without the other, without, that is, an inside and an outside, a tension between constraint and desire. The very word "discourse," in its root sense a "run-ning back and forth," implies the need for such a doubleness. (p. 722)

This kind of analysis allows students to acknowledge their own discourse, and the ideology embedded in it, while beginning to critique their ideology through an encounter with a quite different discourse. It recognizes the potential for conflict, but offers a means of viewing this conflict as an opportunity for critiquing and resisting the "totalizing force" of discourse conventions (p. 727).

Harris and Rosen (1991) also suggested a kind of transforming discourse analysis. Like Spellmeyer, they do not view the writing classroom as a place of initiation into a single academic discourse, but as a place where discourses within and outside the university are critiqued, and where the power of discourse is questioned. Students in one of their early classes, for example, critiqued the power of television to position them as "the masses" by examining their own conflicting desires in relation to television discourse (p. 66). They were thus encouraged to view the writing classroom, and writing itself, as a place where different discourses could be contested.

Schriner (1992) developed another approach to analyzing discourses in a writing program at Northern Arizona University. Recognizing that the program involved not only a variety of cultures (Mexican, Anglo, Navajo, Hopi, Apache, Zuni, and Pais) but also a variety of individuals within these cultures, she designed a curriculum in which students read and critiqued texts that helped them to understand how they both create and are created by their multicultural social realities (p. 98). In one assignment, for example, students were asked to identify which parts of the modern or tribal world the students in *Double Yoke*[5] accepted and rejected, and then to determine whether they agreed with the choices the students made (p. 103). This exercise provided Schriner's students with a means of examining their own cultural conflict, which they wrote about later in the course. One of the interesting outcomes of this pedagogy was the ease with which students moved back and forth between their native discourse and academic discourse, illustrated in an essay in which one student used the metaphor of weaving to describe her educational experience:

> My imagination of becoming a teaching [sic] originated from weaving rugs. Weaving involves a great deal of preparation, discipline, time and energy before a rug can become a finished product. Much like the process of weaving, in order for my dream to become a reality, I had to go through preparation. (p. 109)

This student was able to represent herself in the familiar rhetorical image of a weaver while incorporating this image into an academic discourse that included, rather than excluded, her existence outside the academy.

A final pedagogical example comes from the work of Lisle and Mano (1997), who encouraged students to connect their own cultural diversity with

---

[5]This text by Emecheta (1982) describes the ways Nigerian undergraduates confronted the conflicting demands of the university and their traditional tribal worlds.

the diversity of discourses in the academic community. Students first wrote about the diversity in their cultural and language communities by telling their stories; then they examined the diversity of the communities they were entering in the university through a discourse analysis of diverse academic texts. Lisle and Mano claimed their students were better able to communicate in a diverse social context when they had learned that language conventions are "fluid, contested, and enmeshed in relations of power" (p. 26).

All of these pedagogies require students to conduct their own contrastive rhetoric research. In this sense, they fulfill Kaplan's (1966) early expectation that his "pedagogical devices" would enable students to compare their own rhetoric with the rhetoric of the language they were learning (p. 16). However, students in these contemporary classrooms are not instructed to use their knowledge of contrastive rhetoric to imitate the formal structure of the English language or of academic discourse; rather, they are encouraged to create a discourse in which they can mediate competing rhetorics and conflicting ideologies. This kind of contrastive rhetoric research involves students in a sophisticated understanding of language as "a living, socio-ideological concrete thing [which] lies on the borderline between oneself and the other" (Bakhtin, 1981, p. 293) and helps them create a new, mestizo language that negotiates these borders.

But this understanding of language is not easily acquired, as anyone who has attempted the preceding pedagogies will admit, because we cannot develop a cookie-cutter design that will work in every classroom. We can learn from others' successes and failures, and we can understand the general principles that inform our students' acquisition of a new language or discourse, but we are still experimenting with ways to apply this knowledge. We are all—compositionists, linguists, and students—exploring unfamiliar territory. It is not an easy process, and the results are not uniformly successful. But if we are committed to helping students overcome their resistance to writing about conflicting ideologies in an increasingly polarized society, we may need to begin taking faltering steps across this linguistic frontier.

REFERENCES

Anzaldúa, G. (1990). *La conciencia de la mestiza:* Towards a new consciousness. In G. Anzaldúa (Ed.), *Making face, making soul: Haciendo caras. Creative and critical perspectives by feminists of color* (pp. 377–389). San Francisco: Aunt Lute Books.

Bakhtin, M. M. (1981). Discourse in the novel. In M. Holquist (Ed.) & C. Emerson & M. Holquist (Trans.), *The dialogic imagination: Four essays* (pp. 259–422). Austin: University of Texas Press.

Bakhtin, M. M./Medvedev, P. N. (1978). *The formal method in literary scholarship: A critical introduction to sociological poetics* (A. J. Wehrle, Trans.). Baltimore: Johns Hopkins University Press.

Bergler, E. (1950). *The writer and psychoanalysis.* Garden City, NY: Doubleday.

Berlin, J. (1991). Composition and cultural studies. In C. M. Hurlburt & M. Blitz (Eds.), *Composition and resistance* (pp. 47–55). Portsmouth, NH: Boynton/Cook/Heinemann.

Berlin, J. (1998). Composition studies and cultural studies: Collapsing boundaries. In M. Bernard-Donals & R. Glejzer (Eds.), *Rhetoric in an antifoundational world: Language, culture, and pedagogy* (pp. 389–410). New Haven, CT: Yale University Press.

Connor, U. (1997). Contrastive rhetoric: Implications for teachers of writing in multicultural classrooms. In C. Severino, J. C. Guerra, & J. E. Butler (Eds.), *Writing in multicultural settings* (pp. 198–208). New York: Modern Language Association.

Di Salvatore, J. (1995). *Quelling the norm.* Unpublished essay.

Emecheta, B. (1982). *Double yoke.* New York: Braziller.

Foucault, M. (1977). History of systems of thought. In D. F. Bouchard (Ed.), *Language, counter-memory, practice: Selected essays and interviews* (pp. 199–204). Ithaca, NY: Cornell University Press.

Fox, T. (1990). Basic writing as cultural conflict. *Journal of Education, 172,* 65–83.

France, A. W., & Fitts, K. (1994). Radical pedagogy and student resistance: Can we fight the power? In A. France (Ed.), *Composition as a cultural practice* (pp. 51–61). Westport, CT: Bergin & Garvey.

Giroux, H. (1981). *Ideology, culture, and the process of schooling.* Philadelphia: Temple University Press.

Harris, J., & Rosen, J. (1991). Teaching writing as cultural criticism. In C. M. Hurlbert & M. Blitz (Eds.), *Composition and resistance* (pp. 58–67). Portsmouth, NH: Boynton/Cook/Heinemann.

Kaplan, R. (1966). Cultural-thought patterns in inter-cultural education. *Language Learning, 16,* 1–20.

Kaplan, R. (1988). Contrastive rhetoric and second language learning: Notes toward a theory of contrastive rhetoric. In A. C. Purves (Ed.), *Writing across languages and cultures: Issues in contrastive rhetoric* (pp. 275–304). Newbury Park, CA: Sage.

Kubasak, S. (1988). Doing the limbo with Woolf and Nin—On writer's block. *The Centennial Review, 32,* 372–397.

Leki, I. (1991). Twenty-five years of contrastive rhetoric: Text analysis and writing pedagogies. *TESOL Quarterly, 25,* 123–143.

Leki, I. (1997). Cross-talk: ESL issues and contrastive rhetoric. In C. Severino, J. C. Guerra, & J. A. Butler (Eds.), *Writing in multicultural settings* (pp. 234–244). New York: Modern Language Association.

Lisle, B., & Mano, S. (1997). Embracing a multicultural rhetoric. In C. Severino, J. C. Guerra, & J. A. Butler (Eds.), *Writing in multicultural settings* (pp. 12–26). New York: Modern Language Association.

Lu, M. Z. (1987). From silence to words: Writing as struggle. *College English, 49,* 437–448.

Lu, M. Z. (1992). Conflict and struggle: The enemies or preconditions of basic writing? *College English, 54,* 887–913.

Matelene, C. (1985). Contrastive rhetoric: An American writing teacher in China. *College English, 47,* 789–808.

Nin, A. (1969). *The diary of Anaïs Nin: Vol. 3, 1939–1944.* New York: Harcourt.

Rose, M. (1985). Complexity, rigor, evolving method, and the puzzle of writer's block: Thoughts on composing-process research. In M. Rose (Ed.), *When a writer can't write: Studies in writer's block and other composing-process problems.* New York: Guilford.

Schriner, D. K. (1992). One person, many worlds: A multi-cultural composition curriculum. In J. A. Berlin & M. J. Vivion (Eds.), *Cultural studies in the English classroom* (pp. 95–111). Portsmouth, NH: Boynton/Cook/Heinemann.

Spellmeyer, K. (1989). Foucault and the freshman writer: Considering the self in discourse. *College English, 51,* 715–729.

Stewart, S. (1983). Shouts on the street: Bakhtin's anti-linguistics. *Cultural Inquiry, 10,* 265–281.

Woolf, V. (1954). *A writer's diary.* New York: Harcourt.

4

Doing Global Business in the Information Age: Rhetorical Contrasts in the Business and Technical Professions

Kristin R. Woolever
Northeastern University

Classically, linguistics has been interested in the description of syntactic structure. In 1966, Kaplan's seminal article "Cultural Thought Patterns in Intercultural Education" laid the groundwork for what has become known as *contrastive rhetoric*, a branch of linguistic study that points out the nature of rhetorical differences among cultures, using discourse structure as the site for investigation. Kaplan's article has been especially valuable for teachers in English-as-a-second-language (ESL) classrooms, as it describes culturally based schemas at the paragraph level in written discourse.

Subsequent scholarship has continued this trend, aiming at ESL teachers, and relying heavily on traditional linguistics studies such as articles on coherence and cohesion (Winterowd, 1970; Witte, 1983), T-units (Hunt, 1965), and other discussions focusing on syntactic structure. Recently, a few studies have shifted the focus from the ESL classroom to the business arena (e.g., Connor, 1996; Sherblom, 1997). But even here, the studies remain at the discourse level, primarily describing syntactic structures of specific documents. In 1997, a special issue of the *Journal of Business and Technical Communication*, "How Can We Address International Issues in Business and Technical Communication?" (Driskill, 1997), moved a step beyond discourse analysis to focus more broadly on strategies for communication in the global workplace.

Such a shift is fortuitous. Today's professional communicators could benefit immensely from scholarship in contrastive rhetoric, especially if that work is broadened beyond the micro (discourse) level. Communication in the technical and business arena includes graphics (which have a visual rhetoric all their own), collaborative projects (which require rhetorical strategies of planning as well as executing documents), professional presentations (which include interactions between oral, visual, and written rhetorics), and many other forms of expression where the interplay of culture and communication can create barriers to clarity. Yet, many business and industry professionals are only recently realizing the challenges and opportunities inherent in cross-cultural communication and are looking for ways to address these issues on a macro level. They recognize increasingly that, as technology has made geographic barriers negligible, an understanding of cultural difference in written discourse is essential. Their perspective on contrastive rhetoric is broader than ESL education, the study of discourse structures, and close studies of individual documents.

With the explosive impact of the Internet over the last decade and the astounding rate at which telecommunications is changing our world into a truly "global village," doing business today necessitates crossing national and cultural borders. ALL business is international these days—quite a change from the extreme nationalism of the mid- to late 20th century. This transformation has occurred so suddenly that many of the professionals working in industry are not prepared for the communication issues such a shift demands.

It might help to define what we mean by *culture* in this context and to also clarify the connection between culture, language, and rhetoric. Hoft (1999) offered a brief, to-the-point definition of culture: "Culture is 'the way we do things around here,' and it is 'how people think, feel, and act'" (p. 145). Hoft further suggested—correctly, I believe:

> It is always difficult to differentiate where one culture ends and another culture begins. The most common way to differentiate among cultures, particularly for business purposes, is to use national boundaries. But we know well that within a nation's boundaries, dozens and perhaps hundreds or even thousands of cultures coexist, sometimes peacefully, sometimes not. (p. 145)

Language, as we know, differs among nations and geographic locations, but differences even within the same language are rooted in the cultural history of the native speakers. The French spoken in Paris is quite different from the French spoken in Quebec; the Chinese spoken in Hong Kong differs from the Chinese spoken in the mainland provinces of China; and so forth. Even in the United States, the dialects of the deep South are easily differentiated from the clipped speech of New Englanders.

Rhetoric has many definitions, but for brevity's sake one definition will suffice: Rhetoric is the way we put together language to affect an audience, and each audience has certain expectations of rhetorical structure based on the traditional forms of rhetoric in their culture.

Understanding the relationship of culture, language, and rhetoric is confusing enough within the confines of one culture, but negotiating these relationships across multiple cultures can wreak havoc in the business world when corporations must communicate to international audiences. While communication technology leaps ahead enabling global commerce that demands international conversations, the culturally based world of language is slower to accommodate to the Information Age: Electronic wizardry can provide the opportunities for communication, but only a thorough understanding of the rhetorical contrasts among cultures will allow that communication to be productive. Professionals working in business and industry need to transform their rhetoric to accommodate the multicultural traditions and expectations of people they may never speak to face-to-face. Working with contrasting these rhetorics is a continuous exercise in negotiation.

Meeting the rhetorical expectations of another culture requires more than attention to language. As any technical communicator can tell you, the simple translation of words from one language into another does not guarantee effective communication. The cultural expectations of the target audience may mean that the translator needs to rearrange the information, feature more or fewer visual aids, use different examples, and so forth to avoid ambiguity and to create appropriate contexts for readers to understand the message. Seven main variables affect the way people understand and respond to written material (Hoft, 1995, p. 61):

1. Political variables: trade issues, legal issues, political traditions and symbolism.
2. Economic variables: income, availability of resources, business status.
3. Social variables: age, business etiquette, family and social interaction, popular culture.
4. Religious variables: religious practices, expectations, and beliefs.
5. Educational variables: literacy, learning styles, common body of knowledge.
6. Linguistic variables: official national languages, writing style, reading orientation (left-to-right or right-to-left), pronunciation, syntactic cues.
7. Technological variables: availability, compatibility.

This chapter addresses the need for change in our approach to communicating in the business and technical professions. It is divided into three parts: current issues and strategies in international communication, specific sites of rhetorical contrasts in technical and business communication, and a call for pedagogical reform in higher education to better reflect the actual needs of global industry and to better prepare students to enter these professions.

CURRENT ISSUES AND STRATEGIES
IN INTERNATIONAL COMMUNICATION

Successful international commerce requires cross-cultural communication. For many companies, making a go of their business means taking many layers of rhetorical contrasts into account. Doing so often encourages companies to resort to generalizations that have produced common myths about different cultural groups. But these overgeneralizations, while providing an easy template for marketing products to standard locations, are usually far too rigid in their cultural characterizations: Americans are loud and fast, Germans are abrupt and emphatic, Asians are quiet and polite, and so forth. Popular among corporate communication specialists is the work of Edward T. Hall, an anthropologist and an authority on cross-cultural communication, who divides cultures into two basic types: high context and low context (Hall, 1983, p. 229). In high-context cultures such as China, Korea, Japan, and the Arab countries, the way the message is delivered is as important as the message, and it is actually part of the message. In low-context cultures such as the United States, Germany, Switzerland, and the Scandinavian countries, the meaning is less dependent on such implicit nuances. Instead, communication in low-context cultures depends on explicit written and oral messages. According to Hall, if you are communicating in a high-context culture, you need to pay special attention to traditions and the "niceties" of communication. You may need to begin with paragraphs of polite conversation and compliments to the people involved before you get to the heart of the material. In contrast, in the United States, we plunge right into the main point.

However correct these cultural theories were prior to the Internet and the attendant knowledge revolution, these days most locales have electronic access to cultural "levelers" that have created in the younger generation around the world a similar set of expectations and behaviors. As Kaplan (1987) noted, "It is reasonably well-established that, when two [or more] language varieties come into direct contact, commonly at an economic border, there is a high probability that an intermediate form composed of various elements taken from each of the varieties will develop" (p. 15). So, although we are used to the traditional stereotypes, these standardized characteristics apply to a lesser and lesser degree as disparate communities become more connected via technology. It is also a fact that national cultures are only one of the influences on business: There is increasingly such a thing as "corporate culture" that crosses international boundaries and allows business professionals to share certain rhetorical expectations, if not language. Nonetheless, companies who depend on marketing their products worldwide must still deal with cultural variation in some measure. Their strategies for doing so fall into three categories: globalization, localization, and collaboration.

Globalization

Globalization is a power play where a dominant culture imposes its mores and expectations on the less powerful cultures. Gradually, the world takes on the characteristics of the dominant player, and mass standardization results. In corporate venues, multinational companies who have headquarters in one country and hundreds of branch offices around the world attempt to globalize their operations by using standard practices in their administrative structures, standard processes for conducting business, standard writing styles, and so forth. Reducing language to straightforward words in simple, predictable patterns as devoid as possible of cultural ornamentation allows that language to be translated more easily (often by machine) into equally simple sentences in another language. "Simplified English" is one such means of controlling language that is gaining popularity among technical communicators worldwide. But while this simplicity of rhetoric makes communicating easier at a basic level, it precludes the richness of language and becomes literally mechanistic in style and in meaning. Lost are the valuable connections that could be made if the message were delivered to meet the rhetorical expectations of the audience's culture.

Localization

Some companies believe that the best way to deal with doing business multinationally is to specifically address cultural differences. Localization involves thoroughly researching the culture of a target market and designing products and communication strategies to appeal directly to that audience. Unlike globalization—where culture is downplayed—localization foregrounds the differences and attempts to enhance the effectiveness of communication by aiming at the perceived unique cultural needs and expectations of the audience. Successful localization means that you have to know everything there is to know about the potential relationship between your message and your audience in their home culture. You can make no assumptions.

For example, think of localizing communication as similar to localizing business products to successfully market them in the customer's home territory. As Greg Bathon (1999), president of Contact International, noted, in Mediterranean countries, most of the stores are still mom-and-pop shops with limited shelf space. In Greece, 77% of the people walk to the store and are able to carry their purchases home. In Holland, most people bike to the store, and if your product won't fit into the bike basket, you're in trouble. These are big influences on packaging decisions: conveying the appropriate "message" to meet the needs and expectations of the potential buyer (p. 24).

Developing rhetorical strategies for the target culture requires similar research. Although localization can be effective, when you are dealing with issues of language and rhetoric such research can be prohibitively expensive and take excessive amounts of time. It often requires extensive coordination among staff at various geographic locations and can become a logistical nightmare. At one Massachusetts company, for instance, the process requires a U.S. translation coordinator, a European translation coordinator, a regulatory affairs manager, several in-country reviewers, translation suppliers, document control departments, product managers, publications departments, and print suppliers—not to mention editors, purchasing executives, graphic designers, and so on. All of the work is done in a byzantine process that includes sign-off sheets, collation sheets, print information sheets, translation kits, hard-copy masters, electronic files, Lotus Notes, PDF files, PostScript, and Zip disks (Lavalee, 1999, pp. 12–13).

Collaboration

Increasingly, business is realizing that the best way to deal with cultural differences in communication is neither to deny the contrasts or to focus on them. Instead, companies are beginning to view the middle ground of collaboration as the solution to doing global business in the Information Age. Our maturing global communication technologies enable us to work in virtual teams in the developmental stages of product and information design. By working together in teams that include multicultural and multilinguistic members, business groups can find creative approaches to surmounting cultural differences while remaining appreciative of the complex nuances of contrasting rhetorics. Instead of developing a product in one country and shipping it to another to be redesigned for that culture, or imposing the dominant culture's view, virtual teams can communicate in real time on cross-cultural projects that allow each group member to contribute to the design and bring the best of each culture to the project from the start.

The explosion of electronic information over the last decade clearly indicates that the future of business and technology lies in collaborative communication, and this evolution in business best practices ("e-commerce," if you will) brings with it new requirements for the professions. With communication across cultures so central to productivity, technical and business professionals must be specialists in more than their knowledge area. They must also be communication specialists who are sensitive to contrasting rhetorics in all aspects of their work and learn to negotiate rhetorical strategies that fit each situation.

SPECIFIC SITES OF RHETORICAL CONTRASTS IN TECHNICAL AND BUSINESS COMMUNICATION

The following are areas where the differences in culture-based rhetorical practices and expectations can cause potential miscommunication and embarrassment. This list is by no means exhaustive; it serves only as a catalyst for generating further attention to contrastive rhetoric's effect on the technical and business professions.

Translation

Translation is an obvious area where difference in culture plays a role. The use of syntactic cues (see Hoft's, 1995, "linguistic variables" above) can serve as a good example of the difficulties rhetorical contrasts present writers. A syntactic cue is "an element or aspect of language that helps readers correctly analyze sentence structure and/or identify parts of speech" (Kohl, 1999, p. 149). For example, in English the articles *a, an,* and *the* serve as syntactic cues. Languages such as Japanese and Chinese do not have articles, but they have other syntactic cues that English lacks. Straightforward translation of words from one language to another omits these cues and thus causes difficulties for readers. Other such cues in English are *that; that* + the verb *to be; to* (both as a preposition and as an infinitive marker); correlative pairs such as *either . . . or, both . . . and, if . . . then;* punctuation such as hyphens, commas, and parentheses; and so on (Kohl, 1999, p. 150).

Illustrations

Graphics play a large role in international communication because they convey meaning without relying on words. In some documents designed for multinational release, illustrations dominate the text—some contain no words at all. (Think, for example, of the safety instruction cards found in the seat pockets of airplanes.) It is important to bear in mind that different cultures have different levels of visual literacy and often have different associations for what they see—or no associations at all. An area of caution for technical communicators is the use of icons. We tend to assume that certain symbols are universal simply because they are so prevalent in this country. It is worth checking to be sure that the icons you use are recognizable in the target country. The little e-mailbox icon with its red flag, for instance, is mysterious to many Europeans. They don't have mailboxes like that.

Different cultural perceptions can affect the way audiences perceive color in graphics. In the United States, we associate certain emotions with certain colors. We even have fashion entrepreneurs telling people whether they are best suited to fall, winter, spring, or summer colors. But other nations, who do not necessarily have autumn leaves in October, may have totally different associations for and reactions to oranges and browns. Do certain colors have negative connotations? (The color black, for example, is considered elegant for most formal wear, but not for a wedding dress, and the color white is the color of mourning in many Asian countries.)

Numbers

We tend to believe that mathematics is a universal language that transcends the boundaries of culture. However, the way numbers are presented can vary greatly from culture to culture: Representations of dates, times, and orders of magnitude differ widely. Some cultures even use different systems of measurement—a fact which has cost NASA dearly in recent months when a cross-cultural team of engineers working on the Mars orbiter failed to convert measurements for a key spacecraft operation from U.S. units into metric units, resulting in the loss of the $125-million satellite. Table 4.1 contains examples of differences in numerical representations that may cause similar confusion.

Online Communication and Web Page Design

Online communication has become one of the most common methods of communicating worldwide. When working online you should pay special attention to two elements that can cause potential problems for multicultural audiences: language and graphic design.

Language. Because the benefit of online communication is speed, people tend to pare down their language to the essentials when they write e-mail, when they write online help files, or even when they write material for the Web. Such cryptic language can cause confusion for non-native speakers and

TABLE 4.1
Differences in Numerical Representations

Country			Format
Sample date formats			
United States			March 1, 2000
France			1 mars 2000
Germany (official format)			1.Marz 2000
Sweden			00-01-03
Italy (official format)			1.3.00
Sample time formats			
United States			8:35 p.m.
France			20:35
Germany			20.35
Quebec, Canada			20 h 35
Sweden			kl20.35
Venezuela			8:35
Sample magnitude representations			
	One thousand	*One million*	*One billion*
United States	1,000	1,000,000	1,000,000,000
Germany	1.000	1.000.000	1.000.000.000
Sweden	1 000	1 000 000	1 000 000 000

Note. From St. Amant (1999, pp. 25–27).

people from other cultures. The following suggestions may help you avoid miscommunication in your use of language:

- Avoid using acronyms unless you are sure the audience understands them.
- Keep in mind that the word count in English will not be the same as the word count in another language. When designing text for a single screen, remember that what appears as a single-window topic in English may be boosted to multiple windows because of language inflation.
- Make sure that the links in your hypermedia document are understandable to the target culture. Edit the material carefully to ensure that the keywords make sense for contrasting rhetorics.
- Be prepared to change the graphical user interface (GUI) because it may not work in another language. For example, consider the word *speed* in a button on the screen. The German word for speed is *geschwindigkeit*. Even allowing for 30% to 50% expansion of text in translation, the word is larger than the button it captions.

The World Wide Web itself is in the process of addressing issues of cross-cultural communication in response to the changing dynamics of the business community. A statement posted on the Web site of the World Wide Web Consortium says:

> The World Wide Web still has a bias toward English and the Western European writing system. But modern business, research, and interpersonal communication is increasingly conducted in other writing systems and languages. The Web must be enhanced to meet the needs of the global community. (W3C, 1998)

Graphic Design. People who want to create bilingual or multilingual web pages must depend on extensive collaborative efforts between cross-cultural design teams to integrate web interfaces so that they can deliver the same content and maintain the same "look and feel" while targeting different cultures. As Bishop (1998) advocated in his book on international web design:

> If, for example, you visit MSNBC, C/Net, or ZDNET, you will immediately see that everything looks much the same. The content changes, but you get a sense you belong there. . . . If a Web site's pages are not consistent, then they're a bunch of mini-Web sites all lumped together—messy and confusing. (p. 104)

To achieve an integrated look to web design, many designers will suggest keeping the layout simple and avoid cultural icons altogether. But by suppressing audience-specific details in graphics and attempting a universality, there is a danger that the design will become "nonrhetorical," that is, nonspecific to cultural contexts (Chu, 1999).

When designing Web sites that are not bilingual, but are presented in say, English, for a non-Western audience, pay attention to the cultural implications of color, of reading strategies (left-to-right or right-to-left), and of "extras" in design, such as audio and video.

Correspondence

In business correspondence with readers from other cultures, you should be aware of the customs governing the organization and tone of letters and memos—and e-mail as well. One of the most important elements to consider is the degree to which recipients expect power distance, that is, the distance between the highest and lowest members of society (Beamer & Varner, 1994, p. 171). In cultures with a smaller power distance (e.g., the United States), writers customarily attempt to reduce the power distance by using words and phrases that focus on the similarity between sender and receiver:

> Dear Friend,
>
> Because you are one of our valued customers, we'd like to extend you a special offer. Like most of us, you probably worry about money. . . .

But in cultures with a high power distance (Japan, Asia, Arab, etc.), the power distance is emphasized rather than reduced. In these countries, letters are more formal and writers do not attempt to establish a sense of equality. Even the greeting ("Dear Pat" vs. "Dear Dr. Anwar") depends on cultural expectations.

Proposals

Although they are formal in their correspondence, in many high-context cultures people rely on more informal relationships and discussions to establish the foundations and standards for proposals. Because they rely heavily on oral promises, they may thus view as unnecessary and perhaps as offensive the use of written Requests For Proposals (RFPs) or the use of too much background material in the proposals themselves. If these details have already been discussed orally, then reiterating them in writing may indicate a lack of trust or faith.

Professional Oral Presentations

In oral presentations, the audience's cultural background strongly influences not only what you say, but how you say it. Specifically, differences in cultural expectations affect the formality, pacing, and audience behavior.

Formality. In the United States, the best oral presentations are often those where the speaker seems relaxed yet knowledgeable, where there is a certain level of informality to the talk—a natural, conversational style—that suggests confidence and competence. In other countries, professional presentations are often considered extremely formal and off-the-cuff remarks and behaviors that seem unrehearsed may be frowned on. Taking an interactive approach is often not appropriate because the audience assumes their role is to listen to a prepared performance, not to participate during the speaker's portion of the talk. Even writing on flip charts or overhead transparencies may indicate to the audience a lack of preparation.

Pacing. If you are addressing listeners who do not speak your language as their first language, you should speak at a slower pace than you would normally—but not at such a slow speed that you insult the audience. In high-context cultures you should begin the presentation with an exchange of greetings and other social amenities that will allow you to build a social rapport with the audience and gain their trust. These cultures also often expect presentations to proceed in small segments with time for questions after each "chunk." If you plan to deliver your entire speech before stopping for questions, you may be interrupted frequently.

Audience Behavior. In the United States, we believe that eye contact is a means of engaging the audience and keeping their attention. But in some cultures—throughout Asia, for example—direct eye contact is considered disrespectful, and you will find audiences avoiding your eyes by staring at the floor or looking in another direction. Japanese audiences will nod as the speaker talks to indicate that they understand what is being said, not that necessarily agree with the remarks. Another caution: Unless you know the culture extremely well and feel at home in the environment, avoid using humor in the presentation. Humor is often culture-bound, and what is funny to you may be insulting or in poor taste to your audience.

Cross-Cultural Project Teams

Collaborating in cross-cultural teams expands the normal challenge of collaboration significantly. Understanding how to work in groups and how to motivate and reward team members depends heavily on learning the differences between cultures. For example, the low-context cultures in North America and Europe place the greatest emphasis on the needs of the individual, whereas high-context cultures, especially those in the developing world, prize the collective experience more than the individual. It is also important to realize that some high-context cultures do not encourage speaking up or offering overt opinions. Doing so shows disrespect for the hierarchy of the group and overly emphasizes the individual. These differences affect the way groups establish criteria for success, standards of achievement, the decision-making process, and styles of thinking and communicating. Table 4.2 provides some insight into how cultural differences may affect behavior in group collaboration.

TABLE 4.2
Effects of Cultural Differences on Group Collaboration

Behavior	Rationale	Implication
May not respond with a definite "no"	To prevent both parties from losing face	May take on more work than the others in the group
May be reluctant to admit a lack of understanding or to ask for clarification of information	To do so might place the speaker in a position of revealing ignorance	May pretend to understand
May avoid criticizing others	To avoid embarrassing self or others	May not respond critically to other members of group; may avoid confrontation
May avoid initiating new tasks or performing creatively	To avoid making mistakes and appearing foolish	May accept assigned tasks but may not volunteer
May feel discomfort with compliments	To avoid the imbalance between parties that such compliments create	May not seek verbal approval from the supervisor or other group members
May avoid complaining about a product or service	To prevent other party from feeling a sense of failure	May not indicate problems with group members

Note. From Bosley (1993, pp. 51–62).

Ethics

Most business and technical professionals have individual and corporate codes of ethics that are culturally inculcated. In the past, these cultural codes have conflicted in many arenas, causing mistrust, anger, and often loss of business. With the increasing globalization of business and technology, a number of organizations are establishing written codes of ethics for international commerce. For example, William Frederick, a business ethicist, has developed the Moral Authority of Transnational Corporate Codes (MATCC), a code that divides ethical values for multinational corporations into five universal business areas: employee practices and policies, basic human rights and fundamental freedoms, consumer protection, environmental protection, and political payments and involvement. In Switzerland, the Caux Roundtable has collaborated with representatives from Europe and the United States to create an international code based on 13 principles of social responsibility and ethics. The Society for Technical Communication in the United States has developed a national code of ethics for professional technical communicators and is encouraging its use internationally. As the global marketplace gains more prominence among businesses, these codes will help to assure that the moral values of individual cultures will be less likely to dictate ethical behavior in transnational business practices.

CALL FOR PEDAGOGICAL REFORM

Although these changes are revolutionizing the international marketplace, the way we prepare our undergraduate students to enter that marketplace has remained essentially static. Most engineering, business, and science programs in colleges and universities in this country—and indeed around the world— concentrate on teaching the technology rather than on teaching the human communication skills necessary for success in this electronic society. They rely on English departments or other humanities departments to teach the required course (usually only one) in technical communication, or they import communications faculty to guest lecture on the correct forms for writing a proposal, a lab report, or a computer manual. These guest appearances are often thought of as interruptions of the real course content.

Sadly, even in programs devoted to technical communication, courses in C++ (a computer programming language), Framemaker, Java, web page design, and usability abound, but entire curricula omit courses that address the contrasting rhetorics students will invariably confront when they enter the professional world. A web search of 20 master's-level programs in technical communication yielded only 4 programs that offered courses specifically dealing with these issues. And among those 4, 2 were labeled "cultural studies," a rubric that is fuzzy at best and does not indicate whether the course content is anthropological, literary, sociological, or . . . Other curricula included special-topic courses students could take as electives, but no program included multiple courses where students could study contrasting rhetorics, and few had even one such course as a requirement. A similar gap occurred in a search of curricula at 5 of the nation's top business schools and 7 of the top engineering programs. In these professional schools, culture's impact on language is either left to the humanities department to teach within a required writing course, or it is taught under the guise of international marketing (which does not deal with the rhetoric of written discourse).

The disjunction between the rhetorical issues so central to global technology and the current state of pedagogy in business and technical communication classrooms today is astounding. If we are to remain key players in this economy, we need to retool our programs to match the needs of the emerging professional world. It is essential that the way we teach technical communication does not reinforce stasis but enables flexibility in our students' rhetorical approaches. To do so, faculty—whether they are from the sciences, engineering, business, or the humanities—should pay special attention to three critical areas: curriculum design, textbooks, and delivery of course content.

Curriculum Design

Traditionally, undergraduate courses in technical communication (and many master's-level courses as well) have focused more on the definitive "how-to" approach than on the exploratory, analytical approach. Students are taught how to write in various genres: the technical memo, proposal, report, user manual, and so forth. As a result, students move into the work world understanding how to prepare a report that follows a set rhetorical pattern appropriate for the generic U.S. audience: Introduction, Scope of the Project, Discussion, Conclusions, Recommendations, Appendix. But they are rarely taught methods for discovering the nature of genres in situations with multiple cultures and contrasting rhetorical expectations.

For example, when communicating project information from one culture to another, engineers should not assume they need to pull out the standard formats and fill in the blanks. Instead, they should take the time to learn about the people they are communicating to and discuss with them the form that would be most useful for them. It may be a long report, or it may be a series of short memos, or it may be a conversation with key people. They need to have in their repertoire the tools to create any of these forms, but they should not assume that specific genres work in cross-cultural communication. Nonetheless, in all likelihood that is the only approach they have been taught.

In standard technical communication courses across the country, we have privileged the teaching of forms over the teaching of strategies for successfully conveying information. Even though we pay lip service to audience analysis and spend a significant portion of our classes teaching the document planning process, most of us still concentrate on getting students to understand how to write specific types of documents for specific situations, and we are often frustrated to see in our classrooms so many non-native English speakers who do not have the cultural schemas we believe are necessary to produce effective (i.e., English) technical documents.

Although it is true that technical communication teachers have long urged students to inquire about their audiences prior to writing, most of the approaches to doing so depend on rigid forms. The audience-analysis questionnaires students are often asked to complete do not get to the heart of rhetorical difference, nor do they allow writers to explore meaningfully the commonalities and differences among the parties in a rhetorical situation. Instead, they ask the standard questions about education level, familiarity with the product, possible resistances to the information to be conveyed, and so on. The answers to these questions do not help to define the audience's cultural expectations or provide sufficient information to allow for real communication design. Further, most students who complete such questionnaires do so as a rote activity with no incentive to discover information that will determine their own rhetorical choices. They view the results as helpful only to decide how to arrange the standard report components: Should x come before or after y, and should a be expanded while b is shortened?

The key to productive change in our pedagogical methods is to avoid rigid perspectives and assumptions that are culture-bound. Instead, we should provide opportunities for students to analyze rhetorical situations to find many possible approaches to communication, and we should find ways to teach them strategies for choosing the most appropriate approach from among them. Our curricula must be designed to encourage such flexibility: We should focus on technical communication as a method of inquiry and as a means of negotiating among many possibilities rather than as a course in learning standard forms and a specific skill set.

Textbooks

In a study of professional writing textbooks, Miles (1997) found that "most textbooks contain catalogues of decontextualized factoids rather than strategies for understanding cultural differences" (p. 179). Most technical communication textbooks—even those that take an audience-centered approach and purport to address multiculturalism—give primacy to rules for forms that assume a U.S. perspective. When discussing international audiences, most texts relegate the information to a single chapter filled with bland advice such as "consider your audience" and "be sure to do thorough research on your audience's customs." Those books that move beyond these safe statements often present lists of cultural stereotypes that leave no room for real understanding of cultural difference and reinforce myths that do more harm than good. Furthermore, intercultural communication is often discussed in negative terms: Working with non-native speakers is seen as difficult and constrained, rather than mutually beneficial (Miles, 1997, p. 185). In many of these texts, apocryphal anecdotes about miscommunication across cultures take the place of genuine advice on analyzing rhetorical situations. In these instances, nonnative English speakers are viewed as "others," different from and less competent than the English-speaking audience. The oft-repeated story of General Motors suffering major financial losses when they tried to market the Chevy Nova in Venezuela (*no va* means "it does not go" in Spanish) is nothing more than an imagined incident. It certainly paints GM in a negative light and gives little credit to the people of Venezuela, who would not react in such a stereotypic way. There are whole lists of stereotypic dos and don'ts appearing in textbooks: Never touch anyone's head in Asia because the head is where the spirit resides, don't keep business cards in your back pocket in Japan because it is an insult to present someone with a card you have sat on, and so forth.

Textbooks that include such rules offer limited insight into communication genres and practices, and they rely heavily on fixed, limited, and often dated research. In addition, they reinforce stereotypes and encourage the view of Americans as privileged people who must stoop to conform to the quirky customs of other cultures. Largely ignored is the fact that the Internet and other communication technologies have created changes in many cultural attitudes and practices, especially in professional contexts. Cultural expectations are not unchanging, generalized attitudes that apply uniformly to everyone from a particular region. To think so is dangerous.

Rather than reinforcing stereotypes and cementing cultural differences, textbooks should assume that communication can and must be negotiated among people from equally intelligent and equally privileged cultures. The goal should not be to recognize and maintain difference, but to understand contrasting rhetorical practices and collaborate on communication techniques. Textbooks should weave issues of cultural negotiation throughout the chapters, offering methods for approaching communication collaboratively in a global enterprise with common goals.

Delivery of Course Content

For faculty in technical communication classrooms to prepare students to negotiate among contrasting rhetorics, standard teaching practices must change. The traditional method—where teachers stand in front of a class, lecture on standard techniques, ask the individual students to complete a series of assignments, and then assess those assignments on the basis of correct form—is no longer viable. Table 4.3 illustrates some of the differences between methods used for teaching technical communication in the preceding decades and methods that are more appropriate for teaching students in today's international workplace.

As Table 4.3 shows, preparing students to participate successfully in careers where technical communication is essential requires attention to rhetorical choice—specifically, faculty must teach their students that they have multiple choices that must be negotiated to fit particular situations. It should also be apparent that, although methods of inquiry, collaboration, and negotiation should be well supported by traditional skills in writing, the primary emphasis on narrow views of correctness and culturally bound forms will not serve students well in today's multicultural environment.

It is also worth noting here a word of caution. In well-meaning attempts to retool their courses, faculty sometimes make the mistake of equating the teaching of the latest technology with the teaching of the latest communication techniques. Many instructors, caught up in the glamour of high-tech innovations, update their courses by updating their computer equipment and teaching students the latest software. But, as most employers in business and industry will attest, they want employees who can communicate well; they can master the ever-changing tools on the job.

Pedagogical reforms in technical communication are already underway in many classrooms across the United States and in other countries, although they are largely hit-or-miss. A few programs are redesigning their entire curricula, but it is more common that individual faculty members are experimenting with new course designs. Nowhere is there a coherent call for change

TABLE 4.3
Comparison of Teaching Methods

Traditional Practice	Forward-Looking Practice
• Assumes the individual student will work alone to complete assignments • Assumes a homogeneity of culture among students • Assumes students are writing for a U.S. audience • Views non-native speakers as "other" and less competent • Assumes students need to understand the forms of technical communication genres and be able to write them correctly • Assumes that students should use computers as tools for completing assignments • Assumes that teaching publishing tools (software packages such as Framemaker) will prepare students sufficiently for the work world	• Emphasizes collaborative teamwork where students work on projects for cross-cultural situations • Assumes that students come from a variety of cultures and backgrounds and each is equally valuable • Assumes that students will write for many different cultures • Views cross-cultural communication as mutually beneficial in more than a financial sense • Encourages students to discover how to design effective communication suitable for various cultural situations; "correctness" is a relative term • Where possible, teaches in computer classrooms that allow for interactive group work • Uses synchronous communication conferencing with Internet Relay Chat (IRC) and Multi-User Dimensions (MUDs) and its subdivision, MUDs, Object-Oriented (MOOs) • Uses the Internet to connect students with others working on projects around the world • Emphasizes techniques for negotiating communication where no one culture is superior • Assumes that teaching students methods of inquiry and collaboration is primary, teaching tools is secondary

or a generally accepted recognition that such reform is necessary. As the leader in developing programs for technical communication, the United States is well positioned to lead this transformation. But until we can coherently connect the needs of the work world with the practices in our classrooms, we will continue to do a disservice to our students and jeopardize our position as a world leader in the field of technical communication. On the other hand, exploring the relationships among language, culture, and rhetoric—and learning to negotiate the rhetorical contrasts inherent in cross-cultural conversations—will enable productive collaboration between industry and academe, and will transform the way we do business in this electronic information age.

REFERENCES

Bathon, G. (1999). Eat the way your mama taught you. *Intercom, 46*(5), 22–24.

Beamer, L., & Varner, I. (1994). *International communication in the global workplace.* Chicago: Irwin.

Bishop, M. (1998). *International Web site: Use the Web to market your business worldwide.* Scottsdale, AZ: The Coriolis Group.

Bosley, D. S. (1993). Cross-cultural collaboration: Whose culture is it, anyway? *Technical Communication Quarterly, 2*(1), 51–62.

Chu, S. W. (1999). Using chopsticks and a fork together: Challenges and strategies of developing a Chinese/English bilingual Web site. *Technical Communication, 46,* 206–219.

Connor, U. M. (Ed.). (1996). Contrastive rhetoric in professional settings [Special issue]. *Multilingua, 15*(3).

Driskill, L. (Ed.). (1997). How can we address international issues in business and technical communication? [Special issue]. *Journal of Business and Technical Communication, 11*(3).

Hall, E. T. (1983). *The dance of life.* New York: Anchor.

Hoft, N. (1995). *International communication: How to export information about high technology.* New York: Wiley.

Hoft, N. (1999). Global issues, local concerns. *Technical Communication, 46*(2), 145–148.

Hunt, K. (1965). *Grammatical structures written at three grade levels* (Research Rep. No. 3). Urbana, IL: National Council of Teachers of English.

Kaplan, R. B. (1966). Cultural thought patterns in intercultural education. *Language and Learning, 16,* 1–20.

Kaplan, R. B. (1987). Cultural thought patterns. In U. M. Connor & R. B. Kaplan (Eds.), *Writing across languages: Analysis of L2 text* (pp. 9–22). Reading, MA: Addison-Wesley.

Kohl, J. R. (1999). Improving translatability and readability with syntactic cues. *Technical Communication, 46,* 149–166.

Lavalee, N. C. (1999). Localization tips. *Boston Broadside, 55*(3), 12–13.

Miles, L. (1997). Globalizing professional writing curricula: Positioning students and repositioning textbooks. *Technical Communication Quarterly, 6*(2), 179–200.

Sherblom, J. C. (Ed.). (1997). Business communication outside the United States [Special issue]. *Journal of Business Communication, 34*(3).

St. Amant, K. (1999). International integers and international expectations. *Intercom, 46*(5), 25–27.

W3C. (1998). [World Wide Web Consortium Web site]. Available: http://www.w3.org/International/O-CSS.html

Winterowd, R. (1970). The grammar of coherence. *College Composition and Communication, 32*(8), 828–835.

Witte, S. P. (1983). Topical structure and invention: An exploratory study. *College Composition and Communication, 34*(3), 313–341.

5

Contrastive Rhetoric Theory in an Electronic Medium: Teaching ESL Writers to Become <u>Bricoleurs</u> in a Computer-Assisted Classroom

Dené Scoggins
Texas Wesleyan University

What are the differences between English-as-a-second-language (ESL) students and native English speakers as they become a part of a computer-assisted classroom? What pedagogies are more effective as ESL students adapt to writing for the Web? I suggest that Derrida's concept of *bricolage* serves as a useful metaphor for talking about the tendency of ESL students to juxtapose first-language (L1) and Western rhetorics as they begin writing for electronic genres. Thus, this chapter explores the coping strategies of ESL students as they become writers for the Web and highlights the ways contrastive rhetoric theory can facilitate this process.

As a teacher exploring computer technologies for English studies, I taught a literature survey course in a computer-assisted classroom with wonderfully productive results. These students—all native speakers of English—had worked collaboratively on Internet hypertext projects, and they took advantage of the juxtaposition of ideas, disciplines, and perspectives that a hypertext will support. For example, a student working on a *Wuthering Heights* hypertext used framesets to organize his own Freudian readings of the dream passages in the novel. A psychology major, he used the project to bring together discourses from his own discipline, the literary text, and his insights about the novel as they related to myth and dreams. He and the other members of the group juxtaposed their different approaches to the novel, bringing together what they knew from their disciplines and what they had explored in their separate research endeavors.

These students' strategies can best be described with Derrida's (1986) conception of *bricolage*. In "Structure, Sign, and Play in the Discourse of the Human Sciences," he privileges the *bricoleur* as

> someone who uses "the means at hand," that is, the instruments he finds at his disposition around him, those which are already there, which had not been especially conceived with an eye to the operation for which they are to be used and to which one tries by trial and error to adapt them, not hesitating to change them whenever it appears necessary, or to try several of them at once, even if their form and their origin are heterogenous. (p. 88)

This group of native speakers had adapted so successfully to writing for the Web because they understood the potential of this new medium for heterogeneous juxtaposition. They also intuited the tension between Western rhetorical expectations, which still rely on linear argumentation and other stylistic conventions for print-based texts, and this new medium's potential for freeplay.

As I began teaching a heterogeneous mix of ESL students and native speakers the following semester, I was able to explore the implications of *bricolage* for contrastive rhetoric theory. Not surprisingly, writing for hypertext encouraged unforeseen experimentation with rhetorical strategies, including the transfer of L1 writing strategies to this new electronic genre (Jones & Tetroe, 1987; Leki, 1991). This easy experimentation with rhetorical conventions for the Web exposed the dominance of Western expectations for print-based texts, even in hypertextual writing, a highly mutable and heterogeneous genre. Yet, I would also argue that students who wrote as *bricoleurs*, applying L1 and Western rhetorics as they seemed appropriate, were most successful as writers. *Bricolage* thus suggests a suspension of the L1 rhetoric, rather than its exclusion from rhetorical choices.

The challenge of this class was the diversity of the students, a mixture of native and non-native speakers of English. We all met together in a classroom lined with computers—students from Syria, Sri Lanka, Russia, Hong Kong, four from Indonesia, and six from the United States. They also represented a wide range of ideologies, including Muslim, Marxist, and Hindu, and the ESL students were in different stages in their acquisition of English. Most important, they brought with them different rhetorical expectations for reading and writing. Many had adapted to Western rhetorics, whereas others had difficulty understanding and applying the rhetorical conventions they encountered in classroom discussion, in literary and academic reading, and in writing for the Web. I had a challenge: to create a learning environment hospitable to such a diverse class, in a computer-assisted classroom.

I abandoned previously successful pedagogies for the electronic classroom because they were ineffective with such a heterogeneous group. For example, this class was resistant to whole-class discussion, despite my efforts to get them involved in speaking to each other. They also resisted any kind of small-group work, for obvious reasons: They were so diverse that they struggled to find points of intersection among themselves. Although the Russian student and a few others responded eagerly to my questions and even attempted to initiate discussion in the class, many of their classmates seemed uninterested or unable to participate. The American students, likewise, tried to engage their classmates in discussion early in the semester but soon gave up interacting with many of the non-native speakers. Stages in language acquisition played a part, with some students struggling to express themselves in English, but diverse cultural and rhetorical practices played a much greater role.

Likewise, online, real-time discussion revealed that the students held different expectations for written discourse and lacked shared interpretive strategies. An interchange on Swift's "A Modest Proposal," for example, came to a halt when two of the Indonesian students insisted that we take Swift at his word. In spite of my prereading introductions that included a discussion of irony, they argued that Swift had taken such care to develop the details of this proposal that he must be serious. Some of their classmates responded in total exasperation. Interchanges such as this were not spaces for learning and exchange; they only exposed the rhetorical and cultural chasm between these students. I never gave up on their developing a learning community, but I began to accept the fact that this was not the semester for dynamic classroom discussions.

I had to abandon many of my discussion-driven strategies for the computer classroom and recognize that success is not always measured by performance in the classroom. Rather, in independent research projects, the students could use their own cultural backgrounds and individual rhetorics as a backdrop for their analyses of literary texts. These students would create thoroughly researched hypertexts for the Internet, which presented new and interesting challenges for these diverse writers.

Much has been written about the potential for hypertext as a new genre in an entirely new medium (Anderson, 1998; Bolter, 1991; Charney, 1994; Johnson-Eilola, 1994; Landow, 1992; Rouet, Levonen, Dillon, & Spiro, 1996; Slatin, 1991; Sutherland, 1997). Hypertexts can support close reading and validate the student's argument, juxtaposed as it is to the "authoritative" text. Thus, hypertexts allow students to draw connections and juxtapose contradiction in a kind of *bricolage*. However, this new genre does not escape the conventions of a print-based culture. As Derrida (1986) pointed out, "one calls *bricolage* the necessity of borrowing one's concepts from the text of a heritage which is more or less coherent or ruined" (p. 88). In other words, a new discourse or genre never escapes the language and structure of older forms. The hypertext opens up new possibilities for play and may violate boundaries of genre and fixed lines between disciplines, but as a text-based genre, it must be described with the terms borrowed from print-based expectations, even as it opposes them.

Likewise, ESL writers cannot be expected to abandon L1 rhetorics for a Western rhetoric. Although contrastive rhetoric studies have traditionally focused on the "interference" of L1 writing strategies (Jones & Tetroe, 1987), I would argue that the electronic medium of hypertext suggests a kind of *brico-lage*, a juxtaposition of L1 and Western rhetorics. Many writers in my class had to distinguish, for the first time, their L1 rhetorics from a Western rhetoric of argumentation where writers take an authoritative stance on interpretation. Rather than abandoning their L1 rhetorics for a new one, however, those who were successful held the two suspended, even in their contradictions, and were ready to use one or the other when rhetorically appropriate. As Jones and Tetroe (1987) suggested, successful planning skills from the L1 are regularly transferred to L2 writing tasks. This class's abandonment to the freeplay possi-bilities of the Web thus challenged my own tolerance for heterogeneity in a text-based medium and also offered a new metaphor for discussing the trans-ference of L1 rhetorics to L2 writing tasks.

The class's first hypertext, a frameset of Dante's *Inferno*, revealed the stu-dents' coping strategies, some more successful than others, as they learned to write for the Web. Malek, for example, found connections between his expe-rience as a Syrian Muslim and Dante's worldview. Backed by careful research, he argued that Western critics have ignored the obvious influences Arabic writers had on Dante's own conceptions of hell and purgatory. As Ostler (1987) and Kaplan (1988) have discussed, the Koran and other religious texts are the primary influences on Arabic writing and its stylistic attention to bal-ance and symmetry. This student thus used the hypertext's potential for juxta-posing texts to validate Islamic descriptions of spiritual journeys, largely ignored by Dantean scholars. He recognized the rhetorical expectations for the assignment because he was able to bridge his previous rhetorical expectations for literature, largely based on Arabic texts, and this Western, Christian text.

Likewise, Ellen successfully recognized the rhetorical expectations for this project. A student from Indonesia, she drew conclusions about Dante's state of mind as he begins to notice the shortsightedness of his guide, Virgil:

> Start from Canto XXI, we can see that Dante is starting to have fears and doubts towards Virgil. Dante realizes the fact that there are a lot of changes from the time Virgil visited the Hell until this second visit. Virgil visited the underworld before the crucifixion and prior to the Harrowing of Hell (Inferno IX, 22–27; XII 34–35) and the broken bridge of the sixth bolgia is new to him. He doesn't know about it until the end of Canto XXIII (133–136) that all the bridges are destroyed at the Harrowing of Hell. The truth about his lacking of information

appear when they meet the malebranche and the malebranche try to trick them by giving the wrong information. Dante's fear doubled at that time because Virgil doesn't want to admit his shortage of information. He also doesn't like his authority as a guide being questioned, in addition he has an overconfidence in himself. These all really terrified Dante. Dante realizes if they keep on going like this, they will end up dead like the frog and the mouse in the Aesop fable.

Ellen based her analysis on her own expectations for an authority figure, a guide such as Virgil, and highlighted the deviations from those expectations within the text. She also used the tools of citation and close reading to make her argument that Dante is slowly losing confidence in his guide in Canto 23.

More important, I would suggest that as a *bricoleur* Ellen took advantage of her L1 rhetorical strategies by privileging the fable as an important narrative technique (Erbaugh, 1990). In relating the fable of the frog and the mouse to Dante's state of mind, she intuited the significance of this image to the rest of the canto. Dante refers to this image of a drowning mouse and frog finally snatched up by a hawk to describe his fear of the malebranche devils and their treachery. Yet, as an intuitive reader using the tools at hand, specifically those from her L1 literary background, Ellen reveals the greater significance of the fable to the narrative context.

Sajee, a student from Sri Lanka, likewise took an interpretative stance as she examined Dante's arguably romantic depiction of Ulysses' trip beyond the boundaries of the unknown:

> I feel that Dante has a great amount of respect for this Greek hero, despite his actions against Troy. Dante himself is exploring through the world of the unknown. His travel through hell could be compared to that of Ulysses. The main reasons may be different, yet the underlying similarity is that both men are searching for knowledge beyond what is expected of humans. There are too many people in the world who are afraid of taking chances and who will discourage people who do, and I feel these are the same people who are often unsatisfied with their life. Dante shows us in an indirect way that you may encounter hardships and it is sometimes worth taking chances if it means to fulfill a dream that you have always wanted. It is true that you may have to sacrifice certain things and people, yet if it will make you more happy to take the chance than not, why shouldn't you? I believe that the only regret that Ulysses has is that he died before he could explore everything he wanted, not the fact that he ended up in Hell.

Drawing on her own experience with "taking chances," she explored Dante's attitude toward this shade in Hell. Sajee did not emphasize the contradiction here—that Dante is celebrating Ulysses' exploits when this daring obviously contributed to his eternal damnation—probably because, like Dante, she identified with Ulysses as an explorer of the unknown.

In contrast, other students avoided any kind of argumentative stance in the *Inferno* project. Instead, their coping strategies included a define-and-list approach. Benny, for example, a student from Indonesia, had chosen one of the most pathetic scenes in the *Inferno*, where a starving father, unjustly imprisoned in a tower with his three sons, finally cannibalizes them after their deaths from starvation. Benny, however, avoided any kind of interpretative position in his writing:

> After his sons death, Count Ugolino ate their bodies. Finally, Count Ugolino died not longer after his sons' death.

Instead of commenting on the emotion with which this character relates the tragic story of his death, Benny limited his comments to restatements of the events of the canto.

Benny's define-and-list strategy is not surprising, given the focus on "inter-ference" between L1 and L2 writing expectations in contrastive rhetoric stud-ies (Jones & Tetroe, 1987). For example, recent research indicates that ESL students, especially those students whose rhetorical background includes a respect for authoritative texts, often have difficulty recognizing the rhetorical function of a genre (Belcher, 1995; Erbaugh, 1990; Johns, 1995). The choices Benny made may be explained by his own cultural experience, which prohibits any student assertion of interpretation. Moreover, his matter-of-fact statement of what was said, rather than an interpretation of this monologue in the con-text of Dante's work, resembles Connor's (1984) findings that Japanese stu-dents consistently scored lower in their ability to distinguish "perspective" in a text, compared to Spanish and English speakers. As Connor explained, "use of perspective . . . permits one to explicitly distinguish the writer's point of view from points of view taken by others mentioned in the text" (p. 253). Most likely, Benny did not recognize rhetorical aspects of the text such as "per-spective" and was uncomfortable with the argumentative expectations for the writing task. Thus, he was unable to take advantage of the kind of *bricolage* made possible by hypertexts. His work became an electronic version of foot-notes where people and dates are explained, where redundant plot summaries are provided. In this case, his L1 rhetoric was at odds with the Western rhetor-ical expectations for the assignment, and he was unable to bridge the two.

Moreover, I argue that Benny's attitudes, specifically his orientation to learning English, must also be taken into account when we explain his unsuc-cessful attempt to write for the Web. Schneider and Fujishima (1995) explained that a student's orientation to a new language can be integrative (students are motivated by an interest in the language and become active with native English speakers) or instrumental (students are learning the language as a tool for some other goal). Benny's coping strategies were unsuccessful because, unlike other students, he did not seek out the connections between his L1 rhetoric and these new rhetorical expectations. Moreover, as a non-native speaker of English seeking an engineering degree, his orientation to the language was largely instrumental. Not only did he avoid taking an interpretative stance in his writing, but he also resisted the collaborative framework of the project and worked practically alone.

When it was time to assign the final projects, I encouraged experimentation with culturally diverse texts and stressed rhetorical awareness as these writers planned out their arguments. In the previous semester, I had designed the final projects, making sure that each major text from the semester was covered. With this class, however, the more successful work from the *Inferno* project had broken the rules of my prescribed structure. For example, Malek's juxtaposition of Arabic narratives of spiritual journeys with Dante's journey was a successful *bricolage* that allowed him to connect to the Western text from a position of experience. My assignment for the final project thus needed to allow for this kind of juxtaposition of L1 texts and rhetorics with the Western expectations for hypertext.

Several of the students chose to focus on literary texts from their own countries, even if we had not read them during the semester, so I encouraged them to apply the rhetorical strategies we had been practicing all semester to investigate these more familiar texts. I also continued to "guide" students with mandatory meetings outside of class, multiple draft deadlines, and peer review of projects. Many students, however, resisted the collaborative framework of the assignment. Although I strongly encouraged them to find a group of people interested in similar texts, I did allow independent work. It is interesting that many of the students who resisted collaboration were those ESL students who had the most difficulty adapting to the rhetorical expectations of the *Inferno* project. I argue that their choice to work in isolation indicates an instrumental orientation to learning English. Unlike some ESL writers who worked successfully with native speakers in their groups, several did not attempt to bridge the rhetorical and cultural differences between themselves and their classmates.

As we began the final project, I emphasized the rhetorical expectations for their hypertexts in class discussion and individual student conferences. I allowed independent work but encouraged collaboration. Most important, I was flexible about their choices and encouraged them to make connections between their own cultural experiences and literary texts. I gave up any preconceived notions about what the projects would explore and was satisfied to see them making connection as *bricoleurs*, using the tools at hand.

In these final hypertext projects, students who were successful had a clear rhetorical purpose. Malek, the Syrian Muslim, set out to explore "the representation of women in modern Arabic literature, their image versus the reality in the Arab-Islamic culture." At the end of the project, he did admit that he had failed to find what he was looking for:

It was my initial purpose to attempt to break the stereotypes that are reinforced
by literature, but I have found that the literature in general usually attempt to
highlight the negative aspects of society in order for these errors to be fixed.
Unfortunately over emphasis on these negatives undermines the rest of the rich
Arab culture and civilization.

This admission only strengthened his project, however, because it revealed the
ambiguities of gender representation and stereotypes. As he pointed out, many
Arabic writers focus on cultural reform and highlight abuses in society; thus,
their writings can be used by Western observers to reinforce negative stereotypes of the Arabic world. Because Malek had such a clear rhetorical goal, he
was able to discuss the subtleties of the issue and recognize when he lacked evidence for his position.

Malek worked alone, but even more successful projects were produced collaboratively, especially when non-native speakers paired up with native speakers
of English. For example, Sajee, a Hindu from Sri Lanka, worked with an American student on "Women and Motherhood," a site that explores the representations of women in George Sand's *Elle et Lui*, Honoré de Balzac's *Massimilla Doni*
and Buchi Emecheta's *Joys of Motherhood*. This group's choice of texts illustrates
the free-associative mode of these students as they made connections across heterogeneous texts. Sajee thus took advantage of the medium's potential for juxtaposition with framesets, aligning specific passages from *Joys of Motherhood* with
her own analysis of the ideological perspective of the author.

Some students, however, still relied on a define-and-list approach and
avoided taking a rhetorical stance. In a project on 17th-century science,
Benny and Irvan, both Indonesian students, limited themselves to summaries
of dates, biographical information, and factual descriptions of discoveries
made by Galileo and Kepler. By contrast, Marvin, also from Indonesia, successfully explored the relationship of scientific discovery to religious ideology,
using Blaise Pascal's and Sir Isaac Newton's writings to show the metaphysical
motivations of 17th-century scientists.

How does one explain the radically different coping strategies of these students
from similar cultural backgrounds, working in the same collaborative group? First,
it is important to note that Marvin was much more proficient in English than his
collaborators. Stages in the acquisition of English do play a significant role, as
does their expertise as writers in the L1. As Jones and Tetroe (1987) argued, both
successful and unsuccessful strategies will transfer to the second-language task,
and those students lacking planning strategies in the first language will also be
deficient writing in the second language. Yet, adapting to new rhetorical expectations, including a willingness to suspend L1 rhetorics and take a position on
authoritative texts, may be the most telling indicator of these students' success.

Moreover, students most successful in creating hypertexts demonstrated an
active curiosity about the unfamiliar. Ellen, another student from Indonesia,

spent hours at the Harry Ransom Humanities Research Center at the University of Texas at Austin, an archive of printed texts and manuscripts. There, she researched prophecies published during the 17th century and transcribed the unpublished works of three writers: William Lilly, a political astrologer/propagandist; Lady Eleanor Douglas, whose accounts of her prophetic visions were published during and after the Civil War; and Kent Henry, a writer of apocalyptic prophecies during the 18th century. Ellen drew connections between these writers' prophecies and the chaotic political context that informed them. She even provided her own interpretation of the prophecies and clarified obscure terms and references for her audience. Her orientation to the language and, more specifically, to writing for the Web should be described as highly integrative. Moreover, her curiosity about the unfamiliar allowed for a kind of *bricolage*: Using the tools at hand, she created an original hypertext of archived material where she acted as interpreter for these unknown texts.

These students adapted to this new genre—its rhetorical exigencies and its potential for freeplay—by seeking out the unknown, the incongruous, and the faintly familiar. They tolerated a high level of what Rouzie (in press) called the "hypertext uncertainty principle." He explained that writers "must learn to accept the playful slippery conditions of hypertext writing and use it to some effect." As Derrida (1986) pointed out, "there is a *sure* play: that which is limited to the *substitution* of *given* and *existing, present*, pieces. In absolute chance, [however,] affirmation also surrenders itself to *genetic* indetermination, to the *seminal* adventure of the trace" (p. 93). The students who found the greatest success also took the greatest chances in their writing and allowed for the freeplay of heterogeneous ideas within the rhetorical framework of the genre. As *bricoleurs*, they used the tools at hand, including the rhetorics, cultures, and texts to which they had access, to conceive of unusually juxtaposed "authorial" and student texts.

The success of these ESL writers suggests not only an exciting potential for electronic genres in the ESL classroom but also a new metaphor for discussing contrastive rhetoric theory. As *bricoleurs*, these students adapted to the rhetorical expectations for hypertext by learning the tools of close reading and ideological perspective, using them at times and even suspending them when appropriate. Likewise, they were able to use their L1 rhetorics to their own advantage by suspending rather than excluding them from their rhetorical choices. As Kaplan (1987) has argued, "it is the responsibility of the second-language teacher to increase the size of the inventory, to stipulate the sociolinguistic constraints, and to illustrate the ways in which a choice limits the potentially following text" (p. 11). Thus, I would argue that the metaphor of *bricolage* has implications for the ESL classroom since it emphasizes the potential for rhetorical choice in students' writing where L1 and L2 rhetorics interact, rather than clash, during the writing process. *Bricolage* may also expand our investigative model for L1 transference by emphasizing "interaction," rather than "interference" between first- and second-language strategies.

REFERENCES

Anderson, D. (1998). hybrid://literature/cognition/design. *Kairos*. Available: http://sites.unc.edu/
~daniel/hybrid

Belcher, D. (1995). Writing critically across the curriculum. In D. Belcher & G. Braine (Eds.),
Academic writing in a second language (pp. 135–154). Norwood, NJ: Ablex.

Bolter, J. D. (1991). *Writing space: The computer, hypertext, and the history of writing.* Hillsdale, NJ:
Lawrence Erlbaum Associates.

Charney, D. (1994). The effects of hypertext on processes of reading and writing. In C. Selfe &
S. Hilligoss (Eds.), *Literacy and computers* (pp. 238–263). New York: Modern Language Association.

Connor, U. (1984). Recall of text: Differences between first and second language readers.
TESOL Quarterly, 18, 239–256.

Derrida, J. (1986). Structure, sign, and play in the discourse of the human sciences. In H. Adams
& L. Searle (Eds.), *Critical theory since 1965* (pp. 83–94). Tallahassee: Florida State University Press.

Erbaugh, M. S. (1990). Taking advantage of China's literary tradition in teaching Chinese students. *Modern Language Journal, 74*, 15–27.

Johns, A. M. (1995). Teaching classroom and authentic genres: Initiating students into academic cultures and discourses. In D. Belcher & G. Braine (Eds.), *Academic writing in a second language* (pp. 277–292). Norwood, NJ: Ablex.

Johnson-Eilola, J. (1994). Reading and writing in hypertext: Vertigo and euphoria. In C. Selfe &
S. Hilligoss (Eds.), *Literacy and computers* (pp. 195–220). New York: Modern Language Association.

Jones, S., & Tetroe, J. (1987). Composing in a second language. In A. Matsuhashi (Ed.), *Writing
in real time* (pp. 34–57). Norwood, NJ: Ablex.

Kaplan, R. B. (1987). Cultural thought patterns revisited. In U. Connor & R. B. Kaplan (Eds.),
Writing across languages: Analysis of L2 text (pp. 9–21). Reading, MA: Addison-Wesley.

Kaplan, R. B. (1988). Contrastive rhetoric and second language learning: Notes toward a theory of contrastive rhetoric. In A. C. Purves (Ed.), *Writing across languages and cultures: Issues in
contrastive rhetoric* (pp. 275–304). Newbury Park, CA: Sage.

Landow, G. P. (1992). *Hypertext: The convergence of contemporary critical theory and technology.*
Baltimore: Johns Hopkins University Press.

Leki, I. (1991). Twenty-five years of contrastive rhetoric: Text analysis and writing pedagogies.
TESOL Quarterly, 25, 123–143.

Ostler, S. E. (1987). English in parallels: A comparison of English and Arabic prose. In U. Connor & R. B. Kaplan (Eds.), *Writing Across Languages: Analysis of L2 text* (pp. 169–185). Reading, MA: Addison-Wesley.

Rouet, J. F., Levonen, J. J., Dillon, A., & Spiro, R. J. (Eds.). (1996). *Hypertext and cognition.*
Mahwah, NJ: Lawrence Erlbaum Associates.

Rouzie, A. (in press). The composition of dramatic experience: Play as symbolic action in student electronic projects. *Computers and Composition.*

Schneider, M., & Fujishima, N. (1995). When practice doesn't make perfect: The case of a graduate ESL student. In D. Belcher & G. Braine (Eds.), *Academic writing in a second language* (pp.
3–22). Norwood, NJ: Ablex.

Slatin, J. (1991). Reading hypertext: Order and coherence in a new medium. In G. Landow &
P. Delany (Eds.), *Hypermedia and literary studies* (pp. 153–169). Cambridge, MA: MIT Press.

Sutherland, K. (Ed.). (1997). *Electronic text: Investigations in method and theory.* New York:
Clarendon.

CONTRASTIVE RHETORIC
REDEFINED

Ulla Connor
Indiana University at Indianapolis

Broadly considered, contrastive rhetoric examines differences and similarities in writing across cultures. Although mainly concerned in its first 20 years with the writing of English-as-a-second-language (ESL) students at U.S. universities, contrastive rhetoric today contributes to knowledge about preferred patterns of writing in a variety of "English-for-specific-purposes" situations with the goal of helping teachers and students around the world.

The Finnish textlinguist Nils Enkvist, in his 1997 article "Why We Need Contrastive Rhetoric," showed how contrastive rhetoric can be pursued with varying aims and methods within different institutions at universities and in English-as-a-foreign-language (EFL) situations occurring outside these institutions. Among the institutions benefiting from the theories and methods of contrastive rhetoric, Enkvist gave examples from departments of intercultural communication and schools of business. The present volume is the first concentrated effort in the U.S. context to apply contrastive rhetoric in "mainstream" classrooms rather than in ESL and EFL settings only. The chapters in the first part deal with applications in a variety of U.S. college teaching contexts: in mainstream writing courses with international, immigrant, and resident students with English as a second language (Panetta, chap. 1; Bliss, chap. 2; Corbett, chap. 3); in technical and business writing classes (Woolever, chap. 4); and in computer-assisted literature classes with diverse populations (Scoggins, chap. 5). The chapters in the second part of the book suggest new and different issues for contrastive rhetoric to explore, such as gender contrasts (Micciche, chap. 6), the rhetoric of African-American women (Comfort, chap. 7), and "Gaylect"—the dialect of gay men (McBeth, chap. 8).

The goals of this volume are highly consonant with current thinking in contrastive rhetoric. First, the expansion of contrastive rhetoric theories to other than ESL classrooms is consistent with calls for contrastive rhetoricians to widen their horizons to include potential areas of influence. This is difficult for many ESL-oriented researchers who have often felt that they have no influence on mainstream language and composition theories and practices (Matsuda, 1999); yet, it is a liberating movement. Second, contrastive rhetoric welcomes new influences both in theories and in methods. In a book on the subject (Connor, 1996), I discussed how the discipline expanded from its early beginnings as the study of paragraph organization in ESL student essay writing (Kaplan, 1966) to an interdisciplinary domain of second-language acquisition with rich theoretical underpinnings in both linguistics and rhetoric. In a forthcoming publication (Connor, 1999), I discuss changes in contrastive rhetoric thanks to some recent criticisms of the discipline stemming from changes in definitions of culture, literacy, and critical pedagogy. Each of these is relevant to the chapters in the second part of this book. Forces of heterogeneity and homogeneity are debated in treatments of culture; literacy is considered a dynamic social action not limited to written texts; and the standards and norms of writing in English are changing—indeed, the native-speaker norm is no longer considered the only standard. The following brief discussion explains how changing currents in contrastive rhetoric related to these three concepts directly touch the concerns of the three chapters in the second part of this book.

The concept of culture has received a great deal of discussion in applied linguistics in the past few years. Atkinson (1999) provided a comprehensive review of competing definitions as they relate to TESOL. According to Atkinson, two views of culture are competing in TESOL: the "received view" and alternative, nonstandard views. The received view refers to a notion of culture with geographically and often nationally distinct entities, which are relatively unchanging and homogeneous. The alternative, nonstandard views stem from postmodernist-influenced concepts and have evolved from critiques of the traditional, received views of culture. The received view of culture has viewed culture as a homogeneous entity; thus, in 1996 I defined culture as "a set of patterns and rules shared by a particular community" (Connor, 1996, p. 101). A great deal of contrastive rhetoric has viewed ESL students as members of separate, identifiable cultural groups. It is clear that future contrastive rhetoric research needs to be sensitive to the view that writers be seen not as belonging to separate, identifiable cultural groups but as individuals in groups that are undergoing continuous change. Addressing this need, the chapters by Micciche (chap. 6) and McBeth (chap. 8) bring forth the issue of difference in rhetorical styles favored by women and gay men, respectively. Older contrastive rhetoric research reflects the gender blindness of much research in applied linguistics, which usually assumes no gender-based differences in L2 acquisition.

The second concept brought out in this book concerns a change in the way we think of literacy. Literacy today is seen as a sociocognitive dynamic activity rather than a measurable skill. Influential contributors to the new paradigm, as is pointed out in the chapters, have been Fairclough (1989) and Berkenkotter and Huckin (1993), among others. In Fairclough's model, discourse consists of text, discursive practice (production, distribution, and consumption), and social practice. Traditional contrastive rhetoric has included the first two levels, namely textual and discourse analyses, while the third level, social practice—which includes ideology and political power—are newcomers in contrastive rhetorical research, as the chapters in this book aptly point out. Berkenkotter and Huckin's work has focused on the definitions of genre and has been especially influential in describing how writers need to be socialized into genre knowledge; the socialization involves oral conversations in addition to mastering written literacy conventions.

Contrastive rhetoric work that considers literacy as a complex social interaction between writing and speech has examined different expectations concerning the role of socialization (cf. Belcher, 1994; Connor & Mayberry, 1995; Prior, 1995). Comfort's chapter in this volume, titled "African-American Women's Rhetorics and the Culture of Eurocentric Scholarly Discourse" (chap. 7), powerfully describes the similarities between African-American women and second-language learners, as graduate students struggle between "culturally grounded discourses and those of the academy's disciplinary communities" (p. 93).

The third concept, critical pedagogy or discourse analysis, addresses a major question in contrastive rhetoric. It deals with an ideological problem about whose norms and standards to teach and the danger in contrastive rhetoric of perpetuating established power roles. This issue has been raised in postmodern discussions about discourse and the teaching of writing (Kubota, 1999; Ramanathan & Atkinson, 1998). Many critics have blamed contrastive rhetoricians for teaching students to write for native-speaker expectations instead of expressing their own native linguistic and cultural identities. Researchers working in the contrastive rhetoric paradigm have maintained that cultural differences need to be explicitly taught in order to acculturate EFL writers to the target discourse community. Many, including myself, maintain that teachers of English need to teach students the expectations of the readers. We need, at least, to give students an opportunity to choose. The chapters in this volume describe the complexity of decisions about standards, norms, and acculturation. McBeth's chapter, "The Queen's English: A *Queery* Into Contrastive Rhetoric" (chap. 8), argues for the assertion of linguistic and rhetorical differences in gay men's language for the "production of social visibility" (p. 114): "These Queer writers, and others who use Gaylect, share a similar linguistic and rhetorical style that has a recognizable style and a distinguishable sensibility from conventional—what I will venture to call—'Straight' talk" (p. 119).

In summary, the chapters in this volume emphasize new themes in contrastive rhetoric research. On one hand, they show the expansion of the influence of contrastive rhetoric theories beyond the teaching of ESL and EFL writing. On the other hand, this volume points to new influences for contrastive rhetoric in the revision of its goals and methods. Contrastive rhetoric is indeed responsive to new currents in critical thinking such as the growing emphasis on the fluidity of culture and an acceptance of minority Englishes.

For someone who has spent quite a few years in contrastive rhetoric studies, even shaping its theories, it is gratifying to read about the usefulness of contrastive rhetoric in mainstream English classes. Language inquiry, which includes comparison and contrasts, is a place to start learning about the linguistic and cultural habits of individuals.

REFERENCES

Atkinson, D. (1999). Culture in TESOL. *TESOL Quarterly.*

Belcher, D. (1994). The apprenticeship approach to advanced academic literacy: Graduate students and their mentors. *English for Specific Purposes, 13,* 23–34.

Berkenkotter, C., & Huckin, T. N. (1993). *Genre knowledge in disciplinary communication.* Mahwah, NJ: Lawrence Erlbaum Associates.

Connor, U. (1996). *Contrastive rhetoric: Cross-cultural aspects of second language writing.* New York: Cambridge University Press.

Connor, U. (1999). *Changing currents in contrastive rhetoric: Implications for teaching and research.* Manuscript submitted for publication.

Connor, U., & Mayberry, S. (1995). Learning discipline-specific academic writing: A case study of a Finnish graduate student in the United States. In E. Ventola & A. Mauranen (Eds.), *Academic writing: Intercultural and textual issues* (pp. 231–253). Amsterdam: John Benjamins.

Enkvist, N. E. (1997). Why we need contrastive rhetoric. *Alternation, 4,* 88–206.

Fairclough, N. (1989). *Language and power.* New York: Longman.

Kaplan, R. B. (1966). Cultural thought patterns in intercultural education. *Language Learning, 16,* 1–20.

Kubota, R. (1999). Japanese culture constructed by discourses: Implications for applied linguistics research and ELT. *TESOL Quarterly, 33,* 9–64.

Matsuda, P. K. (1999). Composition studies and ESL writing: A disciplinary division of labor. *College Composition and Communication, 50,* 142–164.

Prior, P. (1995). Redefining the task: An ethnographic examination of writing and response in graduate seminars. In D. Belcher & G. Braine (Eds.), *Academic writing in a second language: Essays on research and pedagogy* (pp. 47–82). Norwood, NJ: Ablex.

Ramanathan, V., & Atkinson, D. (1998). Individualism, academic writing, and ESL writers. *Journal of Second Language Writing, 8,* 45–75.

❦6❦

Contrastive Rhetoric and the Possibility of Feminism

Laura R. Micciche
East Carolina University

Providing teachers with a basis for understanding the differing linguistic and social communities their students occupy, contrastive rhetoric theory (CRT) arguably has been a key backdrop for the current politicization of second-language (L2) teaching. Such work, which, on the whole, does not align itself with CRT, has begun to investigate the ways that feminist teaching might enable L2 students to critically examine cultural constructions of gender (Mackie, 1999; Schenke, 1996); the double marginalization of female ESL students by virtue of their "special cultural and linguistic situation" (Cochran, 1996, p. 159); the ideological work of L2 teaching and research (Benesch, 1993; Willett, 1996); the politics of race in ESL classrooms (Ibrahim, 1999); and the relationship between L2 teaching and critical theories (see Pennycook, 1999). The politics and ideology of teaching L2 learners now poses a substantial challenge to pedagogical theories that once narrowly focused on linguistic contrasts among learners. Still emerging, this work allows us to see a transition from an emphasis on writing skills and language acquisition to an acknowledgment of the broader sociocultural implications of teaching and learning English.

CRT offers fertile ground for further developing this transition. However, it needs to be more explicitly articulated as a theory of linguistic *and* politically constituted differences. Furthermore, although CRT has implications for teaching and learning in both L1 and L2 classrooms, it has been articulated solely in the context of L2 classrooms. This limitation, in my view, has functioned to stymie CRT's broader implications, as the rich insights from rhetorical theory, a transdisciplinary field, have not significantly affected its scope and potential. Therefore, this chapter seeks to explain how feminism—a key

79

rhetorical theory of difference—offers a way of expanding the relevance of CRT. Feminist theories of teaching and learning, I argue, offer essential insights for expanding CRT as a sociocultural rhetoric of difference. My aim, then, is to extend CRT beyond L2 studies and to reconfigure its conception of difference through feminist theories that suggest a more dynamic and rhetorical approach to the study of contrasting cultures.

Ilona Leki (1997) wrote that, at times, CRT, despite its explicit focus on cultural differences, may lead to "regressive and limiting, even blinding, stereotypes and unwarranted categorical distinctions among groups" (p. 241). This is due, I would argue, to an overemphasis on *contrastive* discourse conventions and a de-emphasis on the *rhetoric* of discourse. A more explicitly *rhetorical* theory of linguistic and cultural differences would foreground the contextual and historical nature of such studies. It would also examine the motivations underlying the desire to view language users as conforming to "categorical distinctions," such as the perception that Western students write in a linear fashion and Asian students write in a circular one. As it stands, however, the "contrastive" aspect of CRT overshadows the rhetorical by downplaying the contexts and representations of teaching and learning.

Contemporary feminist pedagogical theory views language as a rhetorical practice inflected, though not strictly defined, by cultural difference. Consistent with this view, here I offer not prescriptions for how to apply gender, race, class, and other identity markers to pedagogy, but a set of feminist principles that might guide CRT research. These principles conceive of teaching as a site where contrasting cultures meet and confront differences. I focus on two aspects of feminist theory that suggest directions for articulating a more appropriate—because timely—response to the current politicization of teaching.[1] The two components of feminist rhetorical theory elaborated here are teaching as a politics of representation and pedagogical scholarship as a form of cultural work. Taken together, this focus shows that writing instruction always involves a representation of teacher identities based not only on selected readings, assignments, and assessment procedures, but also on a teacher's cultural identity and students' perception of it. Furthermore, pedagogical research, as I argue in the second section of the chapter, can be viewed as a site through which we make visible cultural truths or values. A cultural work analysis of CRT has the potential to reveal and raise questions about the truths we posit through contrastive studies of linguistic and cultural differences. Overall, this chapter suggests how CRT might account for the contrastive cultures that teachers and scholars occupy and represent in the classroom and the profession.

---

[1]The politicization of teaching can also be seen in the humanities more generally. For work in composition studies, see Bullock and Trimbur (1991), Carton and Friedman (1996), Fitts and France (1995), Miller (1991), and Sullivan and Qualley (1994). Other approaches include those of Delpit (1995), Giroux and McLaren (1989), Graff (1992), and Shor (1992).

TEACHER IDENTITY AND REPRESENTATION

CRT views cross-cultural differences as essential to understanding the rhetorical choices that writers make. A CRT informed by feminist work might begin to problematize the lack of studies about teachers' rhetorical positionings, especially when the teachers are non-native English speakers or minorities within American culture. In L2 classrooms, non-native and minority teachers may come to personify otherness and inauthenticity to students who expect to learn from a "genuine" or "authentic" English speaker.

Professional identity is a result of the complex locations that teachers occupy. It is shaped not only by one's teaching and research agenda, but also by the cultural identities we carry into both arenas. For example, class status, race, native language, age, body type, sexuality, political perspective, and other factors all produce a certain kind of identity. These factors influence the rhetorical choices available to teacher-scholars, sometimes circumscribing the authority and credibility of one's voice and perspective. If CRT seeks to address how rhetorical choices are shaped by cultural locations, then it must begin to investigate the unique standpoints of teachers, especially those who are non-White and non-native. I say "especially" because much research on multicultural classrooms and liberatory teaching assumes that teachers are members of the dominant culture who *bring* diversity to their students, who facilitate the emergence of differences in their classrooms. Compositionist Shirley Wilson Logan (1998) made this point in " 'When and Where I Enter': Race, Gender, and Composition Studies." Prefacing her classroom narrative about identity in the classroom, she wrote: "Unlike what we now call multicultural classrooms, where the teacher usually belongs to the majority culture, in the classroom under consideration here the students are predominantly white and the teacher is a woman of color" (p. 49). Often overlooked in studies of teaching difference, she suggested, is how minority teachers affect the dynamics of power in multicultural classrooms. Often, such classrooms are student-centered—modeled, as many are, after Paulo Freire's notion of problem-posing education—and, in this sense, seek to displace teacher authority. When the teacher is not a member of the dominant culture, however, relinquishing power and authority in the classroom is not so clear-cut.

In her 1991 essay "Feminism and Composition: The Case for Conflict," Susan Jarratt explained the danger of student-centered pedagogies for women. In particular, she wrote about the problems with expressivist pedagogies that decenter power and envision the classroom as a nurturing environment. The problem, she insisted, is that "the complexities of social differentiation and inequity in late-twentieth-century capitalist society are thrown into the shadows by the bright spotlight on the individual" (p. 109). As Jarratt suggested, it is essential that the endorsement of pedagogical theories such as expressivism take into account the varying social locations that affect teacher identity and authority in the classroom. In this sense, *pedagogy* does not refer only to what happens between students and teachers in classrooms. Because a pedagogical theory is a way of positioning oneself in relation to others, pedagogy also refers to the processes of socialization that instruct teachers on how to position themselves in classrooms. This positioning includes emotional, intellectual, and numerous other forms of conduct that shape one's teacher identity (see Luke, 1996; Worsham, 1998). Such instruction in teacher conduct develops expectations, usually unstated, of acceptable classroom behavior—behavior that varies according to background, ethnic identity, and other cultural markers.

It is my view that these varying cultural locations are relevant not only in terms of student language use, but also in terms of teacher identity. Thus, a wider use of the term *pedagogy* offers interesting ways to understand CRT's vision and construction of the teaching situation. That is, up until very recently, CRT research has largely instructed its readers to consider student language an object of study, while subordinating the location and identity of the teacher. This instruction, in other words, has denied the subjectivity of teachers, a move that unfortunately downplays the rhetorical dimensions of language and writing instruction. Although CRT emphasizes how social differentiation creates contrasting linguistic strategies among student writers, the effects of enculturation on learning must be expanded to address how power differentials inscribe the practice of teaching.

For example, it is clear that minority teachers' rhetorical strategies and choices are significantly different from teachers who are members of more privileged cultural locations. Logan (1998) clarified this point: "Black women are especially challenged to teach communication skills in settings where they must often first overcome resistance to their very presence" (p. 56). Such resistance may be due, as bell hooks (1991) explained, to the construction of African-American women as nurturing "mammies" who sustain the lives of others while subordinating their own needs and desires (p. 154). In addition, the intellectual prowess of African-American women is not especially valued or esteemed in our culture. Their very presence in the classroom, then, disturbs conventional notions of "teacher" and, in some cases, comes to embody and stand for difference.

This final point is illustrated powerfully in Cheryl Johnson's (1994) "Participatory Rhetoric and the Teacher as Racial/Gendered Subject." Johnson asked provocative questions about the way students "read" her body and race as a text: "Am I 'read' as a representation of essentialized black womanhood, and if so, what is that 'reading,' and how much do I participate in or contribute to students' ideas about the nature of black women?" (p. 410). While teaching a Black Literature course, she tells of two White students who could not finish the readings by James Baldwin and Gayl Jones due to painful and disturbing memories evoked by both novels. It is interesting that, by imposing their own experiences on the novels, the students were unable to acknowledge the racialized narratives in the texts and, instead, superimposed their own experiences over the authors'. Johnson pointed out that "these white students felt authorized to invoke their own experience in ways that not only 'de-authorized' me but effectively silenced Baldwin and Jones" (p. 415).

The interactions between racial identity, literature, and authority in Johnson's (1994) account highlight the fact that teacher identity is a rhetorical construct. This insight is useful for revisiting CRT because it makes a claim for expanding contrastive rhetoric to include the way teachers are read, the way they come to represent a particular culture or stereotyped figure in the eyes of students. CRT research might begin to ask how these acts of student agency (i.e., reading and representing) challenge and resist teacher authority when the teacher is not White and/or American. The difference of non-native teachers, in other words, often represents a lack of credibility and authority to L2 students. This is not surprising given that, across the globe, "English" and "American" have a metonymic relation to dominance, freedom, and wealth. Surprising, however, is that cultural difference as a factor that inflects the pedagogical situation has not been of much importance to the study of contrastive rhetoric.

I do not wish to suggest that students single-handedly perpetrate the devaluation of minority teachers. Certainly, the teaching profession itself—its history as an elite profession that instructs students in areas of moral conduct and social behaviors as well as in areas of academic content—must be acknowledged as an influential force behind widely circulating representations of teachers (see, e.g., Spring, 1990). In the cultural imagination, teachers are generally envisioned as representatives of "dominant culture" (i.e., White Americans). When the actual teacher contradicts this cultural script, however, we might ask how the teaching profession deals with this disruption of sameness.

Jacinta Thomas (1999), a non-native teacher of English, offered one reply as she explored the way identity matters are relevant not only to the pedagogical situation, but also to the professional. In "Voices From the Periphery: Non-Native Teachers and Issues of Credibility," Thomas explained how her identity as an English teacher and a first-language speaker of Indian/Singapore English often functions to delegitimize her professional credibility. She explained that discrimination against non-native teachers informs hiring practices, her relationships with colleagues who do not always respect her work, student responses to her, and the TESOL organization, which, ironically, represents the interests of non-native learners. TESOL, that is, "stands for" difference—student cultural and linguistic difference, most explicitly—and, as such, one might assume that it would also seek to represent the interests of the very diverse group of people who *teach* (in addition to *learn*) in L2 classrooms. Yet, as Thomas narrates the first time she taught a class of "native speakers of American English," it becomes clear that her lack of confidence as a teacher was as much a product of her non-native identity as of her alienation from the TESOL organization. In fact, the two seem to reinforce one another.

The persistent challenges to her authority have an accumulative effect on Thomas's (1999) self-worth and self-confidence: "This lack of confidence, this uncertainty about one's abilities, is damaging because it sometimes stands in the way of NNSs [non-native speakers] being all that they possibly can be and of realizing their full potential" (p. 10). Non-native teachers' experiences of alienation and self-doubt might be understood, at least in part, as a problem of representation. That is, these experiences raise questions about how difference gets inscribed through social practices like teaching and language use. More specifically, her account forces us to think about who counts as an "authentic" teacher in our classrooms and who represents a "professional" in our disciplines. This point is emphasized when Thomas writes that, after nervously arriving early to scope out the room where she would be teaching native speakers for the first time, "a young woman sticks her head in, stares at me in confusion, walks outside to check the room number, comes in again and asks: 'Is this an English class?'" (p. 5).

The complicated nature of how difference signifies in the pedagogical situation is also at the heart of Marian Yee's (1991) "Are You the Teacher?" Yee, a Chinese woman, reflected on the disorientation her students experience, and sometimes express, when they realize that she is their Composition 101 teacher. When students do not ask the question that is her title—"Are you the teacher?"—Yee reported that it "hovers, unasked, over the desks" (p. 24). Yee's cultural and racial difference becomes a cultural "text" that challenges assumptions about teachers as authority figures, assumptions that do not link authority with difference. Yee found that students were "uncertain how to read these [cultural] narratives when the positions of the characters change: when the outsider *is* the insider, the foreigner now the subject, instead of the object to be assimilated" (p. 28).

The concept of "foreignness," like authenticity, is certainly relevant to CRT as it articulates a theory of differing rhetorical choices and strategies shaped by cultural locations. Authenticity has to do with the assertion of an essential, singular, and defining voice or identity. Because CRT concerns itself with *contrasts* between identities and languages, it has a definite stake in assertions or perceptions of authenticity and resulting exclusions. In other words, a rhetorical study of contrasting language use must address the contradictions between the value placed on contrasts in language studies and the devaluation of researchers and teachers who speak from positions of difference. An obvious first step toward developing scholarship on the cultural location of non-native teachers would be to generate more narratives of non-native teachers' experiences of cultural isolation and rejection in the profession and in classrooms (see Braine, 1999). Also, however, CRT needs to address teachers' cultural differences and how they affect their rhetorical choices as professional teacher-scholars.

CRT, as Ulla Connor (1997) explained, "maintains that language and writing are cultural phenomena. Thus each language has unique rhetorical conventions" (p. 199). By drawing on feminist conceptions of the pedagogical situation, we can see how CRT might expand to address the fact that teaching is a cultural phenomenon affected by social identifications and representations. A more rhetorical CRT, as this section suggests, must address the sites of language learning and the factors shaping it. Focusing on students' linguistic differences, to the exclusion of teacher differences, discourages reflective examinations of professionalism and the way identity differences shape teacher authority and credibility.

TOWARD A CULTURAL WORK ANALYSIS

By focusing on CRT's cultural work, theorists might develop a more rhetorical and reflective theory of linguistic and cultural difference. Cultural work analysis tends toward the rhetorical by uncovering implicit assumptions and the values they imply. Also, however, this form of analysis seeks to make a rhetorical intervention in the way theory gets done by interrogating its motivations, expectations, assumptions, and so forth. The reflective component of cultural work analysis refers to its capacity to reflect back to us the relationship between what we *say* and what our words *do*. Paul Kei Matsuda's (1999) article "Composition Studies and ESL Writing: A Disciplinary Division of Labor" offers a very clear example of what I mean. Matsuda examined and historicized the disciplinary split between composition and ESL language studies. It is interesting that, due to composition's total exclusion of L2 issues and perspectives from scholarly discussions, "it almost seems as though the presence of over 457,000 international students in colleges and universities across the nation does not concern writing teachers and scholars" (p. 699). Considering the current disciplinary imperative to "difference" composition studies, Matsuda's observation rings especially ironic (see, e.g., Gale & Gale, 1999; Jarratt & Worsham, 1998; Panetta, chap. 1, this volume; Sullivan & Qualley, 1994). The cultural work of composition's efforts to make concepts of difference relevant to scholarly, pedagogical, and professional practices sends quite a contradictory message when considering the exclusion of cultural and linguistic *international* differences from these efforts (for an exception, see Severino, Guerra, & Butler, 1997).

Analyzing the cultural work of a discipline, methodology, or theory is a way of reading its production of truths, values, and unstated assumptions. In the context of composition studies, we might say that difference—despite an increasingly globalized rhetoric, influenced, most recently, by postcolonial theory—is predominantly figured in a national context. By examining the cultural work of composition's rhetoric, we see how certain ideas about difference are "naturalized," obscuring contradictions between stated emancipatory goals and the exclusionary politics of difference that Matsuda (1999) brought to light. In the case of CRT, a cultural work analysis can reveal the values and assumptions embedded in the traditional emphasis on linguistic differences and the concomitant desire to reinforce, rather than question, these differences. Such an analysis might also investigate linguistic and cultural biases endemic to the notion of difference as an object of study. In this section, I briefly outline several noteworthy feminist contributions to cultural work analysis—rather than perform one—in order to provide a bit of context and to suggest the potential for CRT research in this area.

Feminism offers a strong model of cultural work analysis, a form of ideology critique that endeavors to unmask and contextualize the interests served by naturalized assumptions and contradictions (Ebert, 1996, especially pp. 5–9). To my knowledge, the term *cultural work* made its earliest appearance in the subtitle of Jane Tompkins' (1985) *Sensational Designs: The Cultural Work of American Fiction 1790–1860*. In this study, Tompkins read neglected works of fiction not because they are great yet undiscovered literary achievements, but because "they offer powerful examples of the way a culture thinks about itself" (p. xi). Her aim, she told us, was to "explore the way that literature has power in the world, to see how it connects with the beliefs and attitudes of large masses of readers so as to impress or move them deeply" (p. xiv). Literary texts, at least in this particular study, are conceived of as "agents of cultural formation" capable of "doing work, expressing and shaping the social context that produced them" (p. xvii, p. 200).

This view of the cultural value of texts also informs Nancy Armstrong's (1987) *Desire and Domestic Fiction: A Political History of the Novel*. In a chapter entitled "The Rise of the Domestic Woman" (excerpted in *Feminisms*, 1991), she argued that 18th-century women's conduct books reveal

> a culture in the process of rethinking at the most basic level the dominant (aristocratic) rules for sexual exchange. Because they appeared to have no political bias, these rules took on the power of natural law, and as a result, they presented—in actuality, still present—readers with ideology in its most powerful form. (1991, p. 895)

The creation of a "feminine ideal"—nourished by conduct books, women's magazines, and, in the 19th century, women's domestic fiction—instructed women in matters of sexuality and body care, domestic labor, and character (modesty, humility, and obedience being capstones of the ideal). Armstrong argued that conduct books "rewrote the female subject" as a subject with no material body.

In 1963, former journalist Betty Friedan analyzed the production of a feminine ideal through a number of mediums, including the 20th-century version of the conduct book: women's magazines. A bestseller and an important, though also limited, consciousness-raising tool for women involved in second-wave feminism, *The Feminine Mystique* argued that women had come to be defined solely in terms of sexuality. Friedan's book detailed the numerous ways in which the feminine mystique became a feminine ideal that wreaked havoc on the inner lives of countless (White, middle-class, heterosexual) women.

Just as these three examples conceive of literary and popular texts as expressions and reproductions of specific cultural logics, I suggest that CRT and its objects of study, methodologies, and unstated assumptions assert unstated truths and cultural values. That is, CRT is important not only for what it appears to *say*, but also for the cultural work it attempts to *do*. Thus, proponents of CRT might begin to ask questions concerning the cultural work of contrastive language studies, of tendencies to project difference onto students while neglecting to comment on teachers' identities, and on the construction of student identity through cross-cultural explanations of writing "behaviors." If CRT is to become a sociocultural rhetoric of difference and, thereby, a more adequate response to the politicization of teaching and learning, then its proponents must begin to assess the cultural work accomplished in its name. That is, rather than placing all of the emphasis on the rhetorical choices of student writers, proponents of CRT should also examine the rhetorical strategies and choices that characterize this theory of difference. By doing so, CRT can begin to address the construction of teacher and student subjectivity through studies of language acquisition. This issue is of particular importance because traditional CRT has tended to further "difference" students through generalizations about language use, effectively eliding differences *among* learners.

CONCLUSION

CRT has the potential to offer what Clifford Geertz (1973) called "thick descriptions" of the contrasting rhetoric of language learners and teachers. Without a more explicit ideological analysis, however, it may never be able to escape its essentialized history. "Contrastive rhetoric researchers," wrote Leki (1997), "have apparently not been very much interested in exploring the ideological implications of their work, and sometimes teachers have been too eager to embrace questionable conclusions of contrastive-rhetoric research" (p. 244). Such conclusions, Leki observed, encourage too-easy simplifications of cultural rhetorics and, strangely enough, the dismissal of difference within particular cultures. Among other things, this chapter has suggested that a recovery of the *rhetoric* in CRT offers renewed potential for examining the desires and motivations underlying the sort of dismissals that Leki found. Also, however, as I argued in the first section of this chapter, the absence of discussions about teacher identity and difference represents a "dismissal" of another order in need of further study.

The feminist principles elucidated here—teaching as a politics of representation and scholarship as a form of cultural work—suggest several ways to expand the research of CRT. While the former principle offers ways of rethinking the concept of difference in relation to teacher identity, the latter argues for the importance of ideology critique in relation to scholarly pursuits. Both emphases highlight the contributions that feminist theory can make to conceptions of language study and difference and, in this sense, signify the possibility of feminism as a theoretical model rather than a cue to simply insert gender into our discussions.

REFERENCES

Armstrong, N. (1987). *Desire and domestic fiction: A political history of the novel*. New York: Oxford University Press.

Armstrong, N. (1991). The rise of the domestic woman. In R. R. Warhol & D. P. Herndl (Eds.), *Feminisms: An anthology of literary theory and criticism* (pp. 894–926). New Brunswick, NJ: Rutgers University Press.

Benesch, S. (1993). ESL, ideology, and the politics of pragmatism. *TESOL Quarterly, 27*, 705–717.

Braine, G. (Ed.). (1999). *Non-native educators in English language teaching*. Mahwah, NJ: Lawrence Erlbaum Associates.

Bullock, R., & Trimbur, J. (Eds.). (1991). *The politics of writing instruction: Postsecondary*. Portsmouth, NH: Boynton/Cook.

Carton, E., & Friedman, A. W. (Eds.). (1996). *Situating college English: Lessons from an American university*. Westport, CT: Bergin & Garvey.

Cochran, E. P. (1996). Gender and the ESL classroom. *TESOL Quarterly, 30*, 159–161.

Connor, U. (1997). Contrastive rhetoric: Implications for teachers of writing in multicultural classrooms. In C. Severino, J. C. Guerra, & J. E. Butler (Eds.), *Writing in multicultural settings* (pp. 198–208). New York: Modern Language Association.

Delpit, L. (1995). *Other people's children: Cultural conflict in the classroom*. New York: The New Press.

Ebert, T. L. (1996). *Ludic feminism and after*. Ann Arbor: University of Michigan Press.

Fitts, K., & France, A. W. (Eds.). (1995). *Left margins: Cultural studies and composition pedagogy*. Albany: State University of New York Press.

Friedan, B. (1963). *The feminine mystique*. New York: Dell.

Gale, X. L., & Gale, F. G. (Eds.). (1999). *(Re)visioning composition textbooks: Conflicts of culture, ideology, and pedagogy*. Albany: State University of New York Press.

Geertz, C. (1973). *The interpretation of cultures*. New York: Basic Books.

Giroux, H. A., & McLaren, P. (Eds.). (1989). *Critical pedagogy, the state, and cultural struggle*. Albany: State University of New York Press.

Graff, G. (1992). *Beyond the culture wars: How teaching the conflicts can revitalize American education*. New York: Norton.

hooks, b. (1991). Black women intellectuals. In b. hooks & C. West (Eds.), *Breaking bread: Insurgent Black intellectual life* (pp. 147–164). Boston: South End Press.

Ibrahim, A. E. K. M. (1999). Becoming Black: Rap and hip-hop, race, gender, identity, and the politics of ESL learning. *TESOL Quarterly, 33*, 349–370.

Jarratt, S. C. (1991). Feminism and composition: The case for conflict. In P. Harkin & J. Schilb (Eds.), *Contending with words: Composition and rhetoric in a postmodern age* (pp. 105–123). New York: Modern Language Association.

Jarratt, S. C., & Worsham, L. (Eds.). (1998). *Feminism and composition studies: In other words*. New York: Modern Language Association.

Johnson, C. (1994). Participatory rhetoric and the teacher as racial/gendered subject. *College English, 56*, 409–419.

Leki, I. (1997). Cross-talk: ESL issues and contrastive rhetoric. In C. Severino, J. C. Guerra, & J. E. Butler (Eds.), *Writing in multicultural settings* (pp. 234–244). New York: Modern Language Association.

Logan, S. W. (1998). "When and where I enter": Race, gender, and composition studies. In S. C. Jarratt & L. Worsham (Eds.), *Feminism and composition studies: In other words* (pp. 45–57). New York: Modern Language Association.

Luke, C. (Ed.). (1996). *Feminisms and pedagogies of everyday life.* New York: State University of New York Press.

Mackie, A. (1999). Possibilities for feminism in ESL education and research. *TESOL Quarterly, 33,* 566–572.

Matsuda, P. K. (1999). Composition studies and ESL writing: A disciplinary division of labor. *College Composition and Communication, 50,* 699–721.

Miller, S. (1991). *Textual carnivals: The politics of composition.* Carbondale: Southern Illinois University Press.

Pennycook, A. (Ed.). (1999). Critical approaches to TESOL [Special issue]. *TESOL Quarterly, 33( ).*

Schenke, A. (1996). Feminist theory and the ESL classroom not just a "social issue": Teaching feminist in ESL. *TESOL Quarterly, 30,* 155–159.

Severino, C., Guerra, J. C., & Butler, J. E. (Eds.). (1997). *Writing in multicultural settings.* New York: Modern Language Association.

Shor, I. (1992). *Empowering education: Critical teaching for social change.* Chicago: University of Chicago Press.

Spring, J. (1990). *The American school 1642–1990: Varieties of historical interpretation of the foundations and development of American education.* New York: Longman.

Sullivan, P. A., & Qualley, D. J. (Eds.). (1994). *Pedagogy in the age of politics: Writing and reading (in) the academy.* Urbana, IL: National Council of Teachers of English.

Thomas, J. (1999). Voices from the periphery: Non-native teachers and issues of credibility. In G. Braine (Ed.), *Non-native educators in English language teaching* (pp. 5–13). Mahwah, NJ: Lawrence Erlbaum Associates.

Tompkins, J. (1985). *Sensational designs: The cultural work of American fiction 1790–1860.* New York: Oxford University Press.

Willett, J. (1996). Research as gendered practice. *TESOL Quarterly, 30,* 344–347.

Worsham, L. (1998). Going postal: Pedagogic violence and the schooling of emotion. *JAC: A Journal of Composition Theory, 18,* 213–245.

Yee, M. (1991). Are you the teacher? In M. Hurlbert & M. Blitz (Eds.), *Composition and resistance* (pp. 24–30). Portsmouth, NH: Boynton/Cook.

7

African-American Women's Rhetorics and the Culture of Eurocentric Scholarly Discourse

Juanita R. Comfort
Old Dominion University

I could speak fluently, but I could not reveal.
—Michelle Cliff (1985/1998, p. 31)

The academic experience can either empower or silence. It empowers through the inclusion of content which speaks to the breadth of human experience; it silences through the exclusion of those outside the mainstream.
—Sidney Ribeau (1997, p. 23)

A moth is drawn to the light and is ultimately consumed by it. I do not want graduate school to be such an experience for me. The question hovers: how close to the light can I get and not be drawn into destruction? I must be cautious. I must resist impulse. I must survive, wings and spirit intact.
—Maya, a doctoral student

It was about 8 years ago, when I was a doctoral student at a large, predominantly White, Midwestern university, that I began to seriously consider how the discourses of the academy I was poised to enter would reprioritize my life as an African-American woman in midlife. Well beyond the course papers, examinations, and dissertation required by my program in rhetoric and composition, I could envision the range of conference papers, journal articles, chapters in collections, book manuscripts, and other texts that I would need to produce in order to secure tenure and promotion at a future institution and the recognition of colleagues in my discipline.

As I moved through my program, I got to know other African-American women around the university who were also thinking seriously about their situations in the academy. We found that we had much in common. As mainly middle-aged women, we recognized the considerable measure of expertise and wisdom that we brought to our programs, acquired from rich work experiences and substantial social roles. We had been accorded a significant level of authority and respect for our creative thinking and the ways in which we expressed ourselves. These "givens" of our extra-academic lives led us to expect that becoming scholars and professional writers would positively impact the social spaces we had already passed through and would likely return to after earning our degrees. We especially wanted our work to be understood, appreciated, and purposefully engaged by our adult children, friends, colleagues, and community-based constituencies to which we were committed— to make a difference in the lives of people we cared about. Of course, we were also excited about the prospect that our eventual scholarly production might contribute substantially to the conceptual advancement of our fields. It might even be possible, we imagined, to actually help reconstruct some of the academy's traditionally marginalizing discourses so that they would bring non-White and nonmale experiences and standpoints like ours to a more central location within our disciplines—in effect, as the saying goes, "using the Master's tools to dismantle the Master's house."

We students saw our tenure in graduate school as a time for learning how to bring our extra-academic talents, experiences, and linguistic resources to bear on our writing in order to assert an effective yet distinctive authorial presence. It was therefore difficult for us to accept that it was in our best interest to make our graduate-school writings conform, without significant alteration, to the discourse conventions of academic prose, as required by instructors, examiners, and dissertation committees. Because they routinely required us to exclude the very talents, experiences, and linguistic resources that we felt gave us our distinctive perspectives, conventional discourses seemed at times inadequate for serving either our immediate intentions for our subject matter or our long-term visions for development as scholarly writers. In certain respects, we were acquiring a "foreign language" that seemed to prevent us from taking the fullest advantage of the range of resources that were a vitalizing part of our existence. At times, we felt, these conventional discourses forced us to say too much; at times they kept us from saying enough.

The African-American women I got to know often had considerable difficulty eliciting positive judgments about the quality of their work, especially when, in foregrounding perspectives on spirituality, community survival, and human development, they resisted traditional values of rationalism and materialism that underpinned their fields. Disturbingly widespread among my peers was the frustration that no one was teaching them how to write persuasively for disciplinary audiences *while maintaining their own values.* Many complained, over lunches or drinks, that their rhetorical mentoring amounted only to harshly worded critical comments in the margins of their papers which too often passed for genuine guidance, and that such criticism came from faculty who seemed oblivious to their writerly needs and desires. Some of my "forty-something" peers actually took these critiques as insults to their status as mature, intellectual women (they were sometimes several years older than their evaluators) and as a sign that they were not welcome in their programs.

Months of casual conversations with fellow students about these perceptions and issues compelled me to develop formal case studies of some of them, in order to better understand what it meant for them to "write themselves" into the academy. My study participants (whom I have given pseudonyms for this discussion) desired an increased valuation by faculty of their texts and of the social, cultural, and political positions invested in their voices. They were well aware that, historically, the public voices of their sisters have been stifled by the same predominantly White academy that they were now seeking to enter, and they feared that same fate for themselves.

NEGOTIATING CONTRASTIVE DISCOURSES

This discussion uses *contrastive rhetoric* as a reference point for examining some of the challenges that these women faced as they learned to write scholarly discourse in graduate school. Cultural differences are keenly apparent in the juxtaposition of graduate-student writers' culturally grounded discourses and those of the academy's disciplinary communities. Viewing this juxtaposition through the lens of contrastive rhetoric, it becomes possible to see more clearly the issues involved when student writers attempt to integrate cultural perspectives whose roots (in character and rhetorical force) are as much African and feminist as European and masculinist—perspectives that add a sense of integration and synthesis to typically Western approaches of compartmentalization and analysis. The interweaving of such diverse cultural influences shapes a particular kind of writing self whose distinctive rhetorical identity authorizes the content of a text.

Issues regarding the production of scholarly discourse that were raised by my study participants can be usefully examined from the vantage point of contrastive rhetoric. According to Leki (1991) and Connor (1996), contrastive rhetoric theories have perhaps been most commonly understood in terms of their concern with the difficulties that second-language (international) writers often experience in composing texts. Leki reminded us as well that "contrastive rhetoric studies help us to remember that . . . communicating clearly and convincingly has no reality outside a particular cultural and rhetorical context and that our discourse community is only one of many" (p. 139). This cultural dimension is highlighted in Van Dijk's (1997) definition of *discourse* as specific types, classes, or social domains of language use that include the communication of beliefs and interaction in social situations. To understand how discourses function, according to Van Dijk, it is important to consider how the components are ordered and how they may be combined into larger constructs.

The cultural and social dimensions of contrastive rhetoric have led me to consider that there are significant resonances between graduate-level writers who must transition from nonscholarly to scholarly prose and non-native (L1) speakers of English who attempt to write in Standard English (L2). The varieties of English discourses into which many African-American women have been socialized by the time they enter their doctoral programs can differ enough from the prestige discourses of their chosen disciplines that these women's initiation into such discourses resembles in certain respects the distance between a first and second language.

Identifying resonances between nonscholarly discourses as "L1" and scholarly discourses as "L2" helps to frame the dynamic of discourse acquisition taking place for the women of my case studies. To complete the frame, it is important to examine two competing views of acquisition. As it is generally conceived, the concept of *acquisition* comprises an apparently (but, I argue, mistakenly) "neutral" disinterested process of mastering the "rules" of a particular disciplinary discourse. For example, Gee (1987/1998) envisioned acquisition as

> a process of acquiring something subconsciously by exposure to models and a process of trial and error, without a process of formal teaching. It happens in natural settings which are meaningful and functional in the sense that the acquirer knows that he needs to acquire the thing he is exposed to in order to function and the acquirer in fact wants to so function. (p. 53)

He contrasted acquisition with learning,

> a process that involves conscious knowledge gained through teaching, though not necessarily from someone officially designated a teacher. This teaching involves explanation and analysis, that is, breaking down the thing to be learned into its analytic parts. It inherently involves attaining, along with the matter being taught, some degree of meta-knowledge about the matter. (p. 54)

For graduate-student writers, the balance between acquisition and learning, so defined, too often translates into rather truncated demonstrations that they have learned the "rules" of scholarly discourse as presented by a discipline's canonical models, without being encouraged to interrogate or modify those rules for real-world rhetorical purposes, audiences, and occasions. Rhetorically sophisticated students understand that course assignments that produce discourse are never neutral or disinterested. Such assignments condition ways of perceiving and reasoning that, in turn, determine social status and power both inside and outside the discipline. Perceptive students like my study participants (particularly those who, for various reasons, located themselves well outside disciplinary culture) often question the relevance of the classroom as a viable context for the kind of intellectual discourse they wish to engage in.

Meaningful acquisition of scholarly discourse is more than the uncritical assimilation and wholesale reliance on canonical models of disciplinary discourse. Rather than simply substituting one set of raced, gendered, and classed language practices for another, my study participants sought to interweave linguistic resources from diverse facets of their experience—including Eurocentric masculinist discourse—in ways that would help them achieve their own intellectual and social goals. For them, for other African-American women academics I know, and for myself as well, this interweaving of discourses can be usefully characterized as a *negotiation*. The rhetorical exigencies of a given discourse situation, plus the writer's own personal history, beliefs, and values, together define a range of possible roles that she might assume in a text. The voice emanating from that text results from negotiation through a maze of social forces as she accepts some allowable roles and resists others. This image of negotiation has the dual senses of (a) making tradeoffs among valued but competing options and (b) winding one's way through complex cultural terrain. *Negotiation* was a familiar term to my study participants. Indeed, Collins (1990) used a similar image when she asserted that "Black women's lives are a series of negotiations that aim to reconcile the contradictions separating our own internally defined images of self as African-American women with our objectification as the Other" (p. 94).

Particular elaborations of the negotiable dimensions of a discourse constituted "L1" for most of my study participants. By the time they enrolled in their programs, they had acquired a variety of discourses generated within the situations of family, workplace, church community, early education, and other social relationships, all filtered through the statuses of class, gender, ethnicity, generation, and so forth. For some at our predominantly White institution, this range of discourses included the academic discourses normalized within the historically Black colleges and universities where they earned undergraduate and/or master's degrees. For the women who undertook their doctoral educations with the intent of pursuing already well-defined social agendas from the location of an academic career, it became important to negotiate between the discourse practices they brought to their programs and the conventional disciplinary discourses that they found there. Coming to doctoral programs as "L2" learners, they tended to interpret the terms of their writing assignments as a mandate by faculty to "master" features and strategies of Eurocentric masculinist discourses, and further, *they must be socialized in the disciplinary culture that those discourses help to construct*. Sensing considerable danger of self-erasure in such a mandate, some women constructed their assignments as sites of resistance.

STUDENT PERSPECTIVES
ON SCHOLARLY DISCOURSES

I want to turn attention to what my study participants saw in their programs and in their writings. In interpreting my case studies, I found that several key interests motivated these women's efforts to evolve as scholarly writers. One such interest was in helping to ensure that the academy acknowledges its growing diversity in ways that are meaningful to those whose status there for years had been that of the studied, objectified "Other"—which, they perceived, threatened to keep their voices at the periphery of the major conversations of their fields. Through their writings, they desired to negotiate a secure place from which to speak their minds *as* African-American women scholars. Lorrie Ann's comment resonates with several others. She once told me that after 3 years in her political science program, she sometimes asked herself whether an academic career was still relevant to her goals, but that ultimately she was satisfied with her career choice. "Something that we need to do as African Americans is try to someday infiltrate ourselves into [the academic] system to let our voices be heard and at the same time get some legitimacy and credibility for those voices."

My study participants also expressed a deep interest in closing gaps in their disciplines where the contributions of people of color had been overlooked. Tanya related an experience that seems typical of those that propelled other Black women into graduate school. As an undergraduate student teacher in music, she had found that virtually no resources on Hispanic, Asian, or African-American performers were being produced for the music education curriculum in public schools. She recalled an episode that proved crucial to her decision to pursue advanced study:

> I'm standing in front of a classroom that was 95 percent Black, trying to relate Mozart to them. They're looking at me like, "He ain't nothin' but a little short White man playin' on the piano. I don't wanna hear that." But there was no literature out there that I could pull together and say to my students, hey, here's a *Black man* who composed the same type of music Mozart did.

When she mentioned her concerns to her advisor at the time, she was told, "I hear you complaining, but what are you going to do about it? Somebody's got to get in there and write the literature, 'cause *they're* not gonna write it. We already know that." Tanya, now a music historian, concluded, "That's the total reason I came to grad school—to help write that history."

Yet another motivating interest for these women was a desire to use the degree to reinforce their own status as intellectuals, in order to more effectively fulfill the social and political commitments to communities *beyond* the (White) academy that they cared about and desired to influence in some way. Bernice, a literary scholar, envisioned herself making an impact in other areas besides traditional literary scholarship:

> Even though I have some research interests that might not be best served by an historically Black institution like the one I've come from, I've made a decision to teach at a school where I will have a chance to replicate a little bit of what happened to me. . . . I'd like to study how it is that we Black women do all the things we do, like be mothers and work, or be mothers and teach, or teach but also have time to have friendships and form relationships with people. I just don't see any other point. I keep thinking about this wonderful Toni Morrison quote: "If . . . it's not about my community, my village, then it's not about anything."

Lorrie Ann shared Bernice's views. "I know what kind of impact I want to make on the African-American community," she reflected, ultimately perceiving her specialization in political science as an effective way of "shap[ing] my career to help make society better for African Americans. . . . There's a drastic need to have more African-American scholars to educate and broaden the horizons of our Black youth."

My interviews with the study participants generated numerous comments like these. Time and again, they expressed a desire to join their disciplinary communities as the people they were, as agents for change, not as imitations of those they found there. They hoped that opportunities to practice writing in graduate school could prepare them in important ways to achieve their social and political goals. And they knew that if they were ever going to be satisfied with themselves as scholars, those writings had to reflect the totality of their discursively grounded identities. Even though they were students, they were keenly aware of their existence, status, and authority as African-American women prior to and outside the classroom. A major challenge for them was to learn how to balance their faculty's expectations with needs of other audiences whom they ultimately wished to reach. As important as it was for them to emerge from their doctoral programs as certified scholars, it was just as important to be recognized as scholars *on their own terms*—these women did not want to lose their carefully cultivated voices (and the self-concept reflected in those voices) in their quest for enfranchisement in the academy.

A major source of "cultural shock" that some women in my study experienced in their struggle to acquire scholarly discourse was particularly evident in the resistance they met when they tried to shape their writings from distinctively Africentric feminist standpoints. Tanya felt strongly, for instance, that the discursive requirements of her field had stripped away much of her much valued "Blackness" (in terms of worldview rather than color). She claimed that she had not been able to come to the academic table as an

African-American woman scholar, but instead that she had been placed at the
table by her instructors to be(come) what she called a "generic" scholar. "But
it's never really 'generic,'" she argued, "because 'generic' usually means
'White.' In many ways, I feel that they have *neutralized* my color. It upsets me
sometimes, but then I ask myself, 'Are you allowing yourself to be stripped or
are you fighting to retain your identity? And if you're going to fight, how are
you going to fight?'"

If we grant that individuals belong to a number of overlapping discourse
communities, the idiosyncratic nature of each individual's overlapping discourse communities assures her of some uniqueness of voice. Directing writers
solely toward the acquisition of a conventional scholarly discourse, as seems to
be the case for my study participants, can force a writer to suppress the knowledge she needs and desires to make within the boundaries of the academy. Further, student writers driven toward depersonalized discourses may feel that
they are forced to submerge their intuitive abilities to learn through personal
connections. Few of my study participants saw the necessity of separating academic and nonacademic worlds to the radical extent that their disciplines
seemed to require. In fact, several felt that the polarization of discourses was
beginning to create crippling disjunctions in their lives outside of school.

How the discursive conventions and the expectations of academic readers
impact a writer's acquisition/negotiation of a discourse is therefore an important consideration for African-American women graduate students. The influence of a writer's background is an important factor in shaping the "rhetorical
identity" that she constructs within a given text for particular purposes and for
specific audiences. Information from my case studies suggests that many areas
of each participant's background eventually were called into play to enhance
her ability to establish rhetorical agency in her prose and to expand the range
of options and resources she could call on in establishing a credible image of
herself in the eyes of her faculty readers. Further, the self-image constructed by
a writer in her course papers potentially shaped her frame of mind in return, if
we acknowledge that the act of writing is an important means of crystallizing
and reinforcing one's identity. The self-image constructed on the pages of an
academic paper becomes another cultural voice that speaks back to the writer,
reinforcing her sense of herself as a scholar.

Several study participants expressed a strong belief that they were more
controlled by conventional discourses than able to take control of them, but
they could rarely find trustworthy advice about how to take such control. It
seemed to these women that almost every cultural negotiation they would
attempt was deemed "extracurricular" by their instructors, something to be
practiced outside the parameters of their writing assignments, if it at all. Maya,
for example, admitted that she often assumed the burden of writing two papers
for many assignments—one to express herself in a culturally negotiated way
and one to meet what she perceived to be the rather limited expectations of

her professors. Students in several of the disciplines represented in my study said that culturally negotiated writing was never invited, and that they ran the risk of being penalized for attempting to incorporate such writing into their coursework.

When the music historian, the political scientist, the secondary educator, and the Slavic language specialist, and (to a somewhat lesser extent) the folklorist, the literary scholar, and the rhetorician of my case studies attempted to write on subjects in their fields from vantage points of spirituality, sensuality, maternal awareness, or other locations that encouraged a breaking down of boundaries, their papers were likely to be returned with pointed marginal comments and low grades. One instance stands out vividly. Alice, a former military officer who held two master's degrees, nervously showed me a graded course paper that had been returned with line after line crossed out in red ink and her instructor's words penned in between the lines. She apparently was not even allowed to keep her title; that too had been crossed through and reinscribed. Alice lamented, "My professor stated in his evaluation of me that he wasn't impressed with my writing. He *couldn't* have been—he didn't give me a chance to *write* my writing!"

For Black women trying to write not only as students but also as "insurgent intellectuals," to use a term coined by hooks and West (1991), the negotiation of a critical consciousness may further be complicated by their awareness, as expressed by Collins (1990), that "oppressed groups are frequently placed in the situation of being listened to only if we frame our ideas in the language that is familiar to and comfortable for a dominant group. This requirement often changes the meaning of our ideas and works to elevate the ideas of dominant groups" (p. xiii). While Belanoff (1994) focused primarily on issues of class and gender in her study of divergent literacies, I believe her points are just as applicable as Collins' in terms of race and other cultural factors. Belanoff reported that some scholars believe students must master what she called "conventional academic literacy" in order to continue their educations and careers. Further proponents of this position believe that the acquisition of such language is "the most significant intellectual task of students" (p. 256). As Belanoff reads proponents of conventional academic literacy, participation in the academy's knowledge-making enterprise requires using the dominant language of the academy, which carries the power and the respect of the academy's dominant Eurocentric, masculinist factions. If writers wish to wield disciplinary power, it is reasoned, they must "use" discourses invested with power. Those who choose not to, run the risk that their voices will not be heard. Even as the *content* of scholarship opens up, its *discursive rules* do not. As Belanoff articulated this viewpoint, "Although women, minorities, and Third World thinkers and writers are increasingly integrated into course content, the language with which one writes about them should not be altered" (p. 264).

MENTORING STUDENTS
IN SCHOLARLY DISCOURSES

Graduate faculty who hold the previously cited view often present their students with a dilemma that, according to my study participants, those faculty *fail to help them resolve*. The very fact that a prestige disciplinary discourse is invested with power implies that that discourse also subjugates in order to maintain that power. If the rules that underpin a discourse of power work to objectify, marginalize, and oppress the non-White and the nonmale, then a Black female writer who cannot appropriate or challenge those rules is left to participate in her own objectification, marginalization, and oppression. Without the insightful guidance of faculty mentors, the graduate-student writer alone carries the burden of surviving the discourse without becoming consumed by it.

Rhetorical options employed by these writers often attempt to resist such domination, with varying degrees of success. My work suggests that these options range from total compliance with the values and expectations of students' evaluative readers to almost total resistance to them. For example, some participants admitted to imitating the dominant discursive models of their fields so that their work might satisfy their readers' expectation for a "neutral" tone. They felt a sense of discomfort in using this option, however, because they realized that these language practices in reality are not "neutral" at all but *re-create the voice of the prevailing (White male) group*. The writings of other participants, at least part of the time, reflected a more moderate ground, having achieved some degree of balance between personal and public voice that worked for them and, if they were lucky, resonated with their instructors' expectations as well. More often than not, however, these women's writings were never quite balanced, and they came away from their work feeling that they had not made any real space for themselves in their discourse communities.

Much of what disciplinary discourses represented to my study participants about rationalism and materialism tended to submerge their own vested interests in the spiritual, personal, and communal aspects of writing. They recognized and valued multifaceted ways of knowing and the creativity that they engendered, and they were deeply concerned that wholesale assimilation into academic habits of mind might cause them to lose their ability to make sense of their own worlds in multiple ways. If, in forming their self-concept, these women were content merely to align themselves with the values and discursive practices of Eurocentric male-oriented disciplinary cultures, then perhaps they would feel less need for the strong acknowledgments of grounding in home and church communities that they were so eager to express. But there *did* seem to be such a need among my participants. So many of the experiences and reference points these women said they wanted to bring to their writing processes were not necessarily validated for them by their instructors as relevant to the discourses of their disciplines. Only occasionally did the women claim to be successful in engaging their faculty as they desired through their papers. Several reported that their attempts to establish self-defined experiences and reference points on their own, both as valid grounding for the positions they take in their papers and as defining aspects of their scholarly identities, had often been met by certain readers with everything from misinterpretation to outright rejection.

When these women complained about the negative connotations associated with readers' responses to their work, they indicated to me that they assessed their ethos as one of underpreparedness, a priori judgments of unworthiness often colored by the same kinds of racist and sexist attitudes that the women had encountered outside the academy. They were concerned about being placed in relationships with faculty readers, yet feeling stymied by rules of engagement established by those readers for the relationship. They were particularly frustrated by their struggle to assess the implicit agenda behind readers' stated expectations. In such situations, they saw themselves as "outsiders within" a status, as Collins (1990) posited, of being let through the academy's door but not being shown the secret handshake that leads to true enfranchisement.

Some participants, of course, could remember teachers in their past who were sensitive, supportive, and interested in learning from the diversity of their students. More often, however, these women had had teachers who (either deliberately or through ignorance) silenced or ridiculed them. They brought with them into their graduate programs the emotional baggage from previous experiences with those teachers. Often, the frustrations left in the wake of those experiences conditioned the women to mistrust most future encounters, desiring to protect from further abuse the self that gets exposed to those readers through their writing. One significant effect on a writer's negotiation of rhetorical identity and the generation of effective ethos becomes a more distanced, impersonal tone that may not ultimately support the writer's desire to infuse the text with her voice.

All of the issues I have raised to this point lead to important considerations for faculty who teach and mentor graduate-student writers. As evaluative readers of student texts, faculty might consider ways in which many of their own (ostensibly "value-neutral") scholarly practices have actually contributed to the marginalization of politically and economically disenfranchised groups within the "conservative culture" of the academy (as characterized by Edward Said, 1982). As subjects to the power of faculty readers to influence their growth as writing scholars, my study participants needed to be able to trust that their professors would wield that power responsibly in bestowing or withholding the authority to voice difference in academic writing. Such trust demands that evaluative readers also understand the extent to which their brand of academic discourse teaches the biases of academic inquiry. These students desired explicit focus on characteristics which close off knowledge and on routes around those closures that can be made from modes that many African-American women rely on in making knowledge through discourse. While schooling students in the conventional discursive rules that even the students themselves believe they will need to acquire to be successful academics, graduate faculty should be prepared to help them to consider more carefully the consequences of internalizing the rules of the "Master's" discourse.

Without such guidance, students are left to draw their own conclusions about their professors' motivations. For instance, Tanya shared a decision she made to fight against her instructors' apparently arbitrary "red pen" critiques. She recalled many opportunities when she wanted to express something in a particular way but felt that there was no way to do it using conventional academic prose. She related one instance that focused on the question of her competence and authority to advance the terminology of her field:

> I was working on a paper about a particular piece by a Black composer, and I found that there was no adequate terminology for what he was doing. None of the terminology that we had in the field would fit this work because the composer did some pretty unconventional things. But my professor wanted the paper to rely on conventional terminology. When I attempted to coin my own terms . . . talk about static! "Where did you get this term from? Why did you use this?" And I replied, "First of all, you don't have a term to explain what I'm talking about." It was like he was questioning whether I was just making up stuff. There are countless scholars who just make up terms! I started to ask him, "Do you really have a problem with the terms you claim I made up, or do you just feel that this music is inadequate? Is that the problem from the get-go? Maybe it's my subject matter you've got a problem with." And essentially I think that's what it was. We had a major falling-out. I didn't have any off-the-wall "supercalifragilistic" kinds of words, you know what I'm saying? If you looked at the music, you knew exactly what I was talking about, based on what I said in the paper. My professor didn't like it, but that didn't stop me from doing it.

Of course, not all of the women in my study had the same amount of experience in writing for academic audiences. Not all had the same level of response to or mentoring in writing that would have made them comfortable users of the discourse strategies of their fields. Not all had had positive teacherly influences at higher levels of education. As with other areas of negotiation, what the writer believes about her effect on readers is important. Where little mentoring is available, and an attitude of "you're on your own . . . either you pass this test or you don't" prevails, it is usually left up to the writer to pick up whatever she can by way of audience assessment, and merely hope that the resulting text works. When evaluations are inconsistent from one paper to the next and one course to the next, it is hard to develop a range of reliable feedback on which to base a comfortable, relatively stable scholarly identity. If there are inconsistencies within the range of each woman's writing experiences, frequent misreadings of rhetorical context and audience expectations, and lack of confidence in who she is supposed to be to her readers, her negotiation of rhetorical identity can break down and the resulting confusion in the paper can negatively influence the reader's opinion of her and her abilities.

Faculty readers might further do more to help writers transcend the traditional dichotomy of academic versus nonacademic discourse. Many African-American women in the academy increasingly desire to compose their texts in ways that encourage interpersonal and intercultural *interaction* with their audiences. In order to feel confident about using all the resources at their command, these writers need the assurance that their readers are cognizant and appreciative of the nuances of other ways of knowing and being that writers bring to acts of composing. Engendering trust at this level also means developing strategies for helping writers exploit effectively their culturally distinct resources in composing texts designed for academically oriented purposes and audiences.

In sum, faculty readers should plan to encounter the texts of their students in ways that make it more likely that genuine communication is taking place between culturally different but equally enfranchised people. It is a matter of reading to understand the writer as well as the text. In the larger scheme of things, the competing cultural discourses that challenged my study participants must be negotiated by graduate-student writers everywhere, within the particular rhetorical contexts of coursework, examination, and the dissertation. These are key settings in which disciplinary discourses, fraught with cultural and political implications, are made to fit the conceptual framework that is already in place in the writer's own mind, and harnessed in the service of the writer's personal, social, and intellectual goals.

REFERENCES

Belanoff, P. (1994). Language: Closings and openings. In K. B. Yancey (Ed.), *Voices on voice: Perspectives, definitions, inquiry* (pp. 251–275). Urbana, IL: National Council of Teachers of English.

Cliff, M. (1998). A journey into speech. In V. Zamel & R. Spack (Eds.), *Negotiating academic literacies: Teaching and learning across languages and cultures* (pp. 31–35). Mahwah, NJ: Lawrence Erlbaum Associates. (Original work published 1985)

Collins, P. H. (1990). *Black feminist thought: Knowledge, consciousness, and the politics of empowerment.* New York: Routledge.

Connor, U. (1996). *Contrastive rhetoric: Cross-cultural aspects of second-language writing.* Cambridge, England: Cambridge University Press.

Gee, J. P. (1998). What is literacy? In V. Zamel & R. Spack (Eds.), *Negotiating academic literacies: Teaching and learning across languages and cultures* (pp. 51–59). Mahwah, NJ: Lawrence Erlbaum Associates. (Original work published 1987)

hooks, b., & West, C. (1991). *Breaking bread: Insurgent Black intellectual life.* Boston: South End Press.

Leki, I. (1991). Twenty-five years of contrastive rhetoric: Text analysis and writing pedagogies. *TESOL Quarterly, 25,* 123–143.

Ribeau, S. A. (1997). How I came to know "In self realization there is truth." In A. Gonzalez, M. Houston, & V. Chen (Eds.), *Our voices: Essays in culture, ethnicity and communication* (2nd ed., pp. 21–27). Los Angeles: Roxbury.

Said, E. (1982). Opponents, audiences, constituencies, and community. *Critical Inquiry, 9*(1), 1–26.

Van Dijk, T. A. (1997). The study of discourse. In T. A. Van Dijk (Ed.), *Discourse as structure and process* (pp. 1–34). London: Sage.

8

The Queen's English: A *Queery* Into Contrastive Rhetoric

Mark McBeth

City College of the City University of New York

When I began a sociolinguistic study of Gay men's language (what I call *Gaylect*) over 5 years ago, my linguistic observations were done in Manhattan, a location that has a historically established and socially/politically organized Queer population. When I returned to that study for this project, I struggled with how I might use contrastive rhetoric theory as a lens through which to understand and discuss Gay men's language. When I compared what I had done in my dialect study with what constrastive rhetoric required, I recognized some problems: (a) Contrastive rhetoric theory is a strongly text-based theory whereas Gaylect is primarily an oral language; (b) contrastive rhetoric deals with cross-cultural comparisons whereas my Gaylect study emerges from a sub-culture–dominant culture comparison; (c) constrastive rhetoric has become pedagogically useful for vocal/visible students, and yet Gay and Lesbian students often remain silent and invisible in the classroom; and (d) contrastive rhetoric relies on some fairly rigid categories for its conception whereas Queer theory resists such taxonomies that normativize people and their actions. Finding myself in a situation in which I think many Queer people often find themselves, I was again asking (yes, once again), "How do I fit in here?" If I were going to find a place in which to situate myself within contrastive rhetoric theory, I would need to negotiate its, and my own, hermeneutic notions; in sum, our stances would need to remain dialogic.

Unlike many of the studies and approaches that Ulla Connor (1996) surveyed in *Contrastive Rhetoric*, her description of Berkenkotter and Huckin's work opened an obvious venue from which to discuss Gaylect: Their approach locates genres of language in "cultures where humans as 'social actors' learn, monitor, and reproduce the content and form of language they deem appro-

105

priate" (p. 128). Connor went on further to explain how useful considering genre knowledge as a dynamic, social activity would be to student learning: "We should examine the processes whereby a student acquires genre knowledge. Such a dynamic approach is represented by contrastive research on the acculturation process into academic discourse communities" (p. 129). Connor's statement about students' developmental process of language learning applies equally well to Gay men, who learn Gaylect as they begin to identify with—as they become "social actors" in—that particular community. Language is socially constructed. Like the L1 students who integrate themselves into the L2 discourse community, men who have not yet introduced themselves into a Gay community must acculturate themselves to the language and linguistic references that exist there.

The rhetorical universe that Gay males inhabit relies on shared lexical, paralinguistic, intonational, and other linguistic usages that differ from dominant speech patterns and, likewise, distinguish their social and rhetorical needs outside of heteronormative situations and against heterosexist, as well as homophobic, paradigms. They make choices about their spoken (and written) language that "produce an effect on an audience" (Purves, 1988, p. 9). Strong linguistic self-awareness and attentiveness to perceived audiences seem to me lessons from which all language users can benefit. Like the English-as-a-second-language (ESL) learner, the Gay man's rhetorical choices indicate distinct attributes of his cultural affiliation and engender certain responses.[1] Unlike ESL learners (who wish to linguistically assimilate), however, these choices do not occur as unconscious linguistic transferences from their primary tongue, but as purposeful acts of resistance to and identification away from a dominant culture. These Gay male speakers make their rhetorical choices to self-identify and resist;[2] they select to differentiate themselves from the dominant linguistic culture as a means of responding to what may oppress them.

An important thing to demonstrate in this study is a definitive Gay male culture. For some readers, this may be stating the obvious, but, before locating a contrastive rhetoric, one needs to designate a culture from which it contrasts and differs. Although I believe Gaylect exists beyond the borders of New York City,[3] I center my discussion to that region (or isogloss) because, first, I can-

---

[1]When L2 learners write in certain rhetorical modes, their teachers, unfamiliar with these modes, question their structures and written strategies. When rallying Gay men carry written signs that read "We're here, we're queer, get used to it," anti-Gay groups often respond derogatorily, for example, "God hates fags." Neither the L2 learners' nor the Gay men's message need be received so negatively if their "readers" were better informed and less misguided.

[2]This is not to deny that Gay men likewise cloak their identity to create spaces of safety. Although this will be part of my discussion, my examples for this piece of writing tend toward self-identity and resistance.

[3]To digress, an interesting point about pronominal gender shift is that it crosses international linguistic boundaries. In Gay bars in Paris, I've heard *il* changed to *elle*, with all of the

not account for the dialectical or rhetorical characteristics that other Gay enclaves may have constructed; second, this is the environment where I live and see these men interact; and, third, this particular urban environment creates unique conditions for a Gay dialect to emerge.

As a friend of mine once descended a bus at the Port Authority terminal, he overheard a disgruntled man complain, "There are too many faggots. Why don't they just put them on an island somewhere?" My friend quickly responded to him, "Ding dong, buddy, we're on the island where *we've* put *ourselves*— the island of Manhattan." Historically, the creation of urban Gay communities began after World War II, attributable to a number of economic and social factors: (a) the increased number of same-sex couples who had met during the gender-segregated times of war and sustained their relationships afterwards; (b) the relaxation of restrictive sexual mores in the United States; and (c) the changes in patterns of housing and geographical mobility attributable to increased financial abilities that resulted in single men and women moving out of their parents' homes (Levin, 1983, pp. 7–8). After World War II, various Gay activist groups within urban environments such as San Francisco and Manhattan emerged, and Queer communities began to develop. Since then, because of national and international Gay and Lesbian civil rights movements, the catastrophic advent of the AIDS epidemic, and the institution in some geographic areas of Gay and Lesbian antibias laws and domestic partnership statutes, Queers have created stronger, more vital communities, where they've established neighborhoods, community centers, churches, libraries, and eating/drinking establishments. In New York City, Gays and Lesbians have highly visible presences in neighborhoods such as Chelsea, the East and West Villages, and Brooklyn Heights. Gay Pride parades occur in Manhattan, as well as the boroughs of Brooklyn and Queens. In short, New York City offers an environment where the Queer community interacts openly and where its members learn to communicate in ways that are geared to their idiosyncratic needs. Their communicative abilities are formed by the specific contexts and topics of their lives. With the concentration of the Gay population, and the relative freedom that allows them to discuss their issues, a language that fully serves and represents the Gay community becomes necessary and inevitable.

This said, recognizing and studying the linguistic uses of Gay men explores their diverse culture and how that alternative culture is expressed. In his study of Filipino Gay speech (or "sward-speak"), Martin F. Manalansan (1995) emphasized

---

accompanying adjectival agreements required in that language, when referring to a male patron (e.g., *Elle est nerveuse* instead of *Il est nerveux*). Miss Thing becomes *Señorita Cosa* in Spanish. Even my Thai friend changes the masculine form of *So wat dee krub* (hello designated to males' use) to *So wat dee ka* (hello designated to females' use). I speculate, in short, that international versions of Gaylect exist. (For further articles on international Gay language, see Gaudio, 1997; Hall, 1997; Livia, 1997; Manalansan, 1995; Ogawa & Smith, 1997; Pastre, 1997.)

the view that this Filipino gay argot and all other types of gay argot are not mere bundles of words idiosyncratically produced by marginalized peoples. Rather, [this linguistic inquiry] is based on this idea that gay argots are linguistic strategies that enable gay men to negotiate and express their unique experiences and views. (p. 250)

This approach to language parallels the perspective of contrastive rhetoric because, as Clayann Gilliam Panetta once wrote to me, "We all make rhetorical choices based on our cultural stance" (personal correspondence, March 1, 1999). So, the context of Gaylect speakers begins to overlap the context of ESL learners: Seeing and hearing the complexities of their lives and language reduces the simplifications that are imposed on them by external forces. For Gay males, these could be societal, religious, medical, and/or political factions; for L2 learners, these could be societal, pedagogic, educational, and/or political factions.[4]

As with any contingency, allowing Gay men to speak for themselves, and then regarding that speech as a significant indicator that provides a means of forming their culture, realizes a more complex understanding of what it means to be Gay. Bakhtin (1981) stated:

The importance of struggling with another's discourse, its influence in the history of an individual's coming to ideological consciousness, is enormous. One's own discourse and one's own voice, although born of another or dynamically stimulated by another, will sooner or later begin to liberate themselves from the authority of the other's discourse. This process is made more complex by the fact that a variety of alien voices enter into the struggle for influence within an individual's consciousness just as they struggle with one another in surrounding social reality. (p. 348)

If the Gay community can begin to internally understand its ways of conveying meaning, to arrive at a stronger ideological consciousness, it will find ways to better express itself to the external forces that oppress it. Likewise, the external forces, those that are willing to listen, will have a better understanding of how to listen and understand the "alien voice" with which they struggle. One can see how the issues of Gay rhetorical issues and the theories of contrastive rhetoric begin to align.

One major hurdle to reviewing Gaylect within the constructs of contrastive rhetoric theory is that this Gay language is predominantly an oral form, whereas contrastive rhetoric is primarily a text-based theory. For the purposes of my discussion, I lay out the characteristics of Gaylect with spoken examples, but then turn to written text in which Gaylect has been used. These existing but

---

[4]The recent debates and policies regarding English-as-a-second-language at open-admission schools, such as City University of New York, play a significant and often damaging political role in students' educational lives.

infrequent incidences of written Gaylect allow a textual analysis of a language that, I would remind readers, is primarily verbal in its daily use. Although this nontextual approach trangresses the traditional rules and purposes of contrastive rhetoric, it also broadens its theoretical possibilities. For the conventional subject of contrastive rhetoric—the L2 learner—this broadened perspective could perhaps recognize more about L2 verbal–rhetorical behaviors. It could further enlighten our views of L2 students as educational participants, leading to better ESL classroom practices.

Beyond the examples I present, a substantial body of research has been done over the past decade on language use within Queer communities. James Chesebro's (1981) collection of essays includes subsections and articles such as "The Social Meanings of the Words Homosexual, Gay, and Lesbian," "Communication Patterns in Established Lesbian Relationships," "Gay Liberation as a Rhetorical Movement," and "Lesbianfeminist Rhetoric as a Social Movement." As seen in these initial studies of "Gayspeak," one can easily recognize the importance of rhetorical constructs to its investigators. This remains true in Jeffrey Springer's (1994) collection *Queer Words, Queer Images* over a decade later. Parallel to many of the contrastive rhetoric studies, these essays explore the rhetoric of Gay political and cultural campaigns and of the rhetorical forces responding to the Gay community. In yet another collection, *Queerly Phrased* (Livia & Hall, 1997), a group of essays surveys the use of Gay language across cultures (i.e., "Linguistic Gender Play Among French Gays and Lesbians," "The Gendering of the Gay Male Sex Class in Japan," "Not Talking Straight in Hausa," and "Hijras and the Use of Sexual Insult"). Overall, these collections of Queer language research indicate a viable rhetorical universe that differentiates itself from a dominant (heteronormative) rhetoric that prefers to keep it linguistically obscured—"Don't Ask, Don't Tell."

Typically, language must provide the required and ample vocabulary for a group's needs and context. The common example given of this phenomenon is the 11 different words for snow used by Eskimos. An analogous incidence of lexical importance in Gaylect is the names for the male genitals. H. Max Austin's (1988) lexicon *gay(s) language: a dic(k)tionary of gay slang* discussed this language function and described difficulties he had creating his dictionary:

> As it turns out, there were four categories simply too big to handle for exhaustive cross-indexing, such as masturbation, with 16 terms. Anal intercourse received 42 entries. This is not the end of the story, however; fellatio pulled in a breathtaking 56 entries. Nevertheless, the overriding champion with the greatest number of entries is—you guessed it—the male member itself, with 36 terms just for penis, an additional 18 for uncircumcised penis, etc. (p. iii)

His entries for the variations on the word *penis* were: beatmeat, black jack, bone, butcher knife, candy cane, cock, dick, dildo, dink, dong, dork, egg roll, fuckmuscle, gun, hose, jackhammer, joint, loaded gun, log, lollipop, meat, pecker, peter, pole, popsicle, prick, samurai sword, schlong, schmuck, schwantz, skinflute, sweetmeat, sword, wang, well hung, wong (p. 32). The vocabulary list for *penis* can also be scanned for the references to ethnicity (black jack, egg roll, samurai sword, schmuck, schwantz), profession (butcher knife, hose, jackhammer, loaded gun), and even culinary preference (candy cane, lollipop, meat, popsicle, sweetmeat). Each of these variants has a special way, and a particular context, in which it is spoken. Likewise, these lexical items for the word *penis* have an ingrained nuance of meaning, whether it be social, semantic, or cultural. Although I've never heard or utilized many of these terms, as an experienced Gaylect speaker I can imagine how they would be incorporated into certain conversations.

During a conversation I once had in a Manhattan Gay bar, one of these terms, *meat*, was incorporated into a sentence for multiple reasons. When I asked a man where his friend had disappeared, he responded, "He went out to get a burger, because he sure wasn't getting any meat here." The man's response performed polysemantic functions: (a) It answered my question; (b) it made a provocative yet clever pun about the burger's meat and the "meat" market (cruising area) that existed in the bar; (c) it told me his and his friend's attitudes about the availability of potential lovers in that bar; and (d) it presented a flirtatious and unassuming proposition to me, which I recognized in the context of our previous conversation. Lexical items in Gaylect are not only created to fill in gaps or replace words that standard language cannot fulfill, but they also are placed in self-created structures for self-created functions; they have rhetorical force. Some of these structures and/or functions become important and emphasized only in the context of Gay culture.

For example, sometimes the cultural aspects of words are created to describe the specialized inclinations of Gay men's desires. The word *queen* is often used within the community to refer to its members. It can at once be disparaging and show internalized homophobia ("He always acts like a big queen") while also demonstrating support and solidarity ("Queens gotta stick together"). It can be compounded with other linking words to make qualifying remarks. Some examples are "rice queen" (a Gay man attracted to Asian men), "snow queen" (a Gay man attracted to White men), "Queen Mother" (a Gay man who takes a social leadership position), and "old, tired queen" (an elderly Gay man). In many cases, the disparaging use of these phrases reveals the racist and ageist, and underlyingly misogynist, problems that exist in the Gay community. (I have, however, heard these terms used endearingly and without malice.) We can see how language use places certain diacritical marks on a culture, like Kaplan's "doodles" (Connor, 1996, p. 157), suggesting certain generalizations that must be revisited as one understands more about that discourse *and* community.

Another discursive influence on the Gay community is AIDS. In a narrative by David Groff (1990) about his HIV testing, he said, "The time had come for me to take the Test, as we gay men call it. 'The Test' is part of our succinct new vocabulary of non-words—PCP, DDI, KS, DHPG, CMV, AZT—all representing either opportunistic infections or treatments for that acronym looming in so many of our lives: AIDS. For years I had wondered which non-word might ambush me and which series of non-words could prolong my life" (p. 47). Groff delivers a concise, moving statement of how the AIDS epidemic has affected the lexicon of Gay language. I know that I am often careful with my use of the word *positive* and the common phrase "Are you positive?" I consider the implications of this once-benign phrase for men whose viral status is questionable or who have had it affirmed. Even with the medical advances for HIV-related diseases, such a simple question could be a painful reminder.

Lexical items not normally considered in contrastive rhetoric theory play a specialized role in Gaylect. Their rhetorical force relies on the communal memory of meaning shared within the Gay male community, and the multiple purposes those meanings may convey—negative or positive, pejorative or affectionate. The locutionary force of a word such as *fag* may take on different meaning depending on the situation in which it is spoken, and the person and their intent from which it originates. Its rhetorical force differs from the intimate surroundings of friends to the unfamiliar neighborhood of strangers. A similar example is the Gay and Lesbian community's reappropriation of the word *queer*. Although still derogatory and insulting for some community members, this term works to envelop a variety of people more inclusively, not only Gay men and Lesbians, but also Bisexuals, Transgenders, and Transexuals. It further does not discount the contributions of genitally "Straight" persons whose ideas resist heteronormativity. The performative quality of these terms has an effect on the audiences that hear them. When one announces "I am Gay" to one's family, it will have some effect on those who listen and, subsequently, on the person who speaks.

The performativity of Gaylect surfaces in many contemporary cultural venues, from television sitcoms to music videos to films. In Jenny Livingston's (1990) docu-ethnography, *Paris Is Burning*, she filmed the lives of Gay men involved in the New York phenomenon of the Ball. A Ball is a gathering of Gay men, mostly African-American and Latino, to compete in different categories of dressing up as the characters present in various social strata: female fashion models, military men, banji boys. Contestants are rated on the authenticity of their chosen character and awarded prizes for their "realness" or credibility as that social presence. The Ball offers these men a place where they can parody the social positions that society will not permit them to assume, and furthermore be rewarded for a "realness" that is unlikely to be commended elsewhere. I use some linguistic excerpts from that film to illustrate Gay men's need to create new meaning-making. The arena of the Ball is a situation that minority Gay men create, and for which they need to likewise create specialized language. In a speech given to the spectators in the movie, the emcee of a Ball states:

You have space to do all that you intend to. Now the categories are **Butch-Queen** one through seventeen and for **the girls** eighteen through 30. As far as all of you not **walking** please realize that we all at one time or another have **lusted to walk** a ballroom floor. So give the patrons or contestants you know a round of **applause for nerve.** Cause with y'all vicious motherfuckers it do take nerve. Believe me. We're not going to be **shady just fierce.**

His speech is charged with Gaylect, and I've put the most prevalent phrases in boldface. This vocabulary and its specialized semantics were created as a means to describe a marginalized phenomenon by a marginalized community. This excerpt describes the event, acknowledges the needs of the audience, and sets the audience's rules of etiquette during the event. Even though "standard" social roles and rules refuse to make positions for these men, and standard language forms offer no appropriate expression, these Gay men create their own roles and rules, and the linguistic forms to express them. Neither the parameters of the available social positions nor the parameters of the available linguistic forms are adequate for their context. As resourceful human beings, these Gay men find new ways to express themselves, socially and linguistically. Bakhtin's (1981) explanation of socially shifting discourse suits both the performative and linguistic acts of these Gay men:

> This process—experimenting by turning persuasive discourse into speaking [role-playing] persons—becomes especially important in those cases where a struggle against such images has already begun, where someone is striving to liberate himself from the influence of such an image and its discourse by means of objectification, or is striving to expose the limitations of both image and discourse. The importance of struggling with another's discourse, its influence in the history of an individual's coming to ideological consciousness, is enormous. One's own discourse and one's own voice, although born of another or dynamically stimulated by another, will sooner or later begin to liberate themselves from the authority of the other's discourse. This process is made more complex by the fact that a variety of alien voices enter into the struggle for influence within an individual's consciousness (just as they struggle with one another in surrounding social reality). All this creates fertile soil for experimentally objectifying another's discourse. A conversation with an internally persuasive word that one has begun to resist may continue, but it takes on another character: *it is questioned, it is put in a new situation in order to expose its weak sides, to get a feel for its boundaries, to experience it physically as an object* [italics added]. For this reason stylizing discourse by attributing it to a person often becomes parodic, although not crudely parodic—since another's word, having been at an earlier stage internally persuasive, mounts a resistance to this process and frequently begins to sound with no parodic overtones at all. (p. 348)

The men who create the Ball and its accompanying language exemplify Bakhtin's theory as nearly a textbook case. Theirs is perhaps crudely parodic because, as of yet, it is not allowed to be anything else. These men's struggle against the image of prescribed manhood and heterosexuality has dynamically stimulated them to create the Ball and its language as a resistance. The struggle between the externally authoritative voice of heterosexism and their internally persuasive Gay voices exposes their lack of position in heterosexist society; thus, the Ball, its awards, and its language constitute a parodic discourse to liberate these Gay men.

These role-playings by Gay men are not limited to the runways of the Balls. Gay men in many diverse situations use the parodying of their positions as a means to negotiate the authoritative voice with the internally persuasive voice. One of those forms of parody that has been named and discoursed is *camp*. Susan Sontag (1966) wrote in her "Notes on Camp": "Obviously, its [camp's] metaphor of life as theater is peculiarly suited as a justification and projection of a certain aspect of the situation of homosexuals" (p. 292). The aspect she refers to is the Gay man's necessity for theater in his life. The relation of drama to language has taken on a major importance in the creation of Queer theories and lives (see Butler, 1990, 1997; Leap, 1996; Sedgwick, 1990). Sedgwick stated:

> The relations of the closet—the relations of the known and the unknown, the explicit and the inexplicit around homo/heterosexual definition—have the potential for being peculiarly revealing, in fact, about speech acts more generall . . . [T]he density of their social meaning lends any speech act concerning these issues . . . the exaggerated propulsiveness of wearing flippers in a swimming pool: the force of various rhetorical effects has seemed uniquely difficult to calibrate. (p. 3)

In other words, the ways in which one performs one's language has a definite effect—a "force"—on the people involved in that language act.

This theater may take on a variety of linguistic and paralinguistic forms that create a drama of role-changing when situations command them: perhaps the hiding of one's flamboyant nature when at the office, or the clever flirtation when signaling potential desire. In Bakhtinian terms, the internal persuasion (the Gay man's voice) and their external authority (the heterosexist environment) interact to stage the context in which both must react to each other. For a politically growing Gay community (Gay male or Lesbian), this means that acts are visible and voices are audible (e.g., "We're here. We're Queer. Get used to it"). Moe Meyer (1994) put it eloquently:

> In the sense that queer identity is performative, it is by the deployment of specific signifying codes that social visibility is produced. Because the function of Camp, as I will argue, is the production of queer social visibility, then the relationship between Camp and queer identity can be posited. Thus I define Camp as the total body of performative practices and strategies used to enact a queer identity, with enactment defined as the production of social visibility. (p. 5)

Although a Gay language performance such as "coming out" may be particularly exemplary, the performativity holds true for non-Queer individuals as well. Imagine the rhetorical results of a student's apologetic admission to his teacher, "I don't have my composition ready for today." Inevitably, the student's act of "coming out" as unprepared will have some effect on the teacher and his or her reaction: anger, poor evaluation, leniency, or concerned inquiry.

Language contributes to the production of social visibility. I further argue that Gay men's recognition of this visibility (audibility) through language, in contrast to the heterosexist linguistic culture in which they live, affects the way they create and present their rhetorical universes. The contrast occurs in the words they choose, the way they turn a phrase, and the way these linguistic features parody their oppression. In a *Village Voice* article on the 1995 Million Man March on Washington, James Hannaham (1995), an out Gay male, recounts his experience (I present this piece in its entirety, because it seems so exemplary as a whole):

> When I heard that at least one very out gay brother I know planned to participate in the Million Man March, I reexamined the rationale I'd built up for resisting, and the march began to sound inviting. Sure, the Nation of Islam denounces homosexuality, I began to reason, but so does the U.S. military. The NOI supposedly has similar "don't ask, don't tell" policy, and some of those brothers have definitely been to prison. Perhaps the NOI's outcry against homosexuality is a case of the lady protesting too much and, as a friend suggests, demanding the g-thing to hide the g-string.
>
> I'm not about discouraging female participation in the spirit of sexism (which the M³ was not doing, contrary to popular belief), but a certain part of me (I'll leave which one to your imagination) is tempted by spectacles involving all-male casts. And as my colleague Lisa Kennedy would say, I'm *sorry*—those NOI paratroopers got it going on, marching around as if they've actually got somewhere to go with their black jumpsuits full of shelf-butt. Lord—excuse me, Allah—have mercy.
>
> Though I'd set my sights on bagging a paratrooper, I discovered that a group organized by the Black Gay and Lesbian Leadership Forum had joined the march, despite not only the NOI's hostility but the quasi-religious overtones of the entire event. So I traded one type of action for another. As Ken Reeves said, after BGLLF introduced him at its pre-march rally as the "openly gay African American" mayor of Cambridge, Massachusetts, "Wherever a million black men are, I'm gonna be there."
>
> Everyone in the group seemed to bring some special flavor—demure students marched next to dreadlocked dshikiboys, suits kissed kinte-capped casuals. As we approached the mall, already teeming with paragons of black masculinity, as well as a smattering of sisters, some of them, I'd discovered earlier, sorta free with their hands, we expected "incidents." I worried that hard-liners would pelt us with rocks and bottles. But at worst, we received confused looks and stares. Of course we had presented ourselves, as the BG&L movement tends to, in an over-

spiritualized and defeminized manner, chanting, "Gay Men—WOOF!—of African Descent!" in order to express our solidarity with the former Arsenio Hall audience members in the crowd swelling around what had suddenly become the Denzel Washington Monument. Only two or three GMADs in the group felt free to join me in adding a snap to the end of the chant.

This was the "coming home" gay black men always write and dance and make films about, and daddy wasn't going to have some sashaying snap queen with a handbag on one arm and a go-go boy on the other barging back into his house. A two-spirited, dreadlocked, ashe chanting afrocentric neomonk Santeria practitioner—he might welcome that. But this ideal of gay black male authenticity sometimes seems too removed from the basic idea that our struggle diverges from our het bros' mostly because we like to get fucked up the ashe.

So when the roughly 100 of our number arrived in a dense cluster on the cold, wet lawn forming a prayer huddle and encouraging those who wished to deliver microsermons of any denomination, I agnostically took the opportunity to get closer to a fellow marcher, one whose insouciant spirit had tempted him to carry a sign saying "I Got Your Man." "Have you got a prayer?" I asked him. As sure as the red flag of the NOI flew above a contingent not 10 feet away from us, he bit me through my shirt. "You don't have to pray for *that*," I informed him.

Though Maya clapped, Jesse failed to enunciate, and Stevie plugged his album, none of them came close to even uttering the word "homophobia," as we'd hoped. The crowd got impatient for the arrival of M^3 impresario Minister Louis Farrakhan, or as we called her, Miss Louise-Farrah Khan. Then, like some aging, addle-brained diva lit professor, she burst onto the podium, greeting us with a hearty "I slam and lick him!" to which we naturally responded, "Why lick him? Slam!"

Self-critical yet self-aggrandizing to the extreme, this stone crazy bitch—after giving us a little lesson in architecture, numerology ("the nine in 19 represents a woman who is pregnant"), and the history of freemasonry—delivered her unsubtle coup de arrogance: "I may have a defect in my character, but there is no prophet mentioned in the Bible without a character defect." What did she mean to imply by that? I'm not perfect, but neither was Jesus, hint, hint? Did someone tie her bow tie a little too tight this morning?

"You can't separate Newton from the Law of Gravity," she went on, grabbing as much as possible for inspiring the proceedings. She was so high on the adulation of her estimated 2 million men in attendance—well, I can identify—that she went off for two and a half hours, straying far and wide with feeble attempts to reprise earlier themes. She spent at least a half hour on a close reading of the word "atonement," unpacking that sucker like a Gucci handbag. The NOI member she'd "cured of AIDS" caused a commotion as we pondered the cause of his original seroconversion. She lost us—and we lost it—when the former virtuoso violinist explained that the "Atone" vibrates at 440 cycles per second, "and how many years have black people been in this country? 440!" And how long is the radio version of RuPaul's "Supermodel (You Better Work)"? 4:40! There you have it, black men of America!

We had to hand it to her, though. White America perceives Farrah Khan as dangerous, though it generally considers the phrase "dangerous black man" redundant. Sure, Louise is a lunatic and we don't trust her as far as we could throw her. Nevertheless, she managed to pull off a much-needed if only precursory step in the self-determination of black American men. She did not order her thugs to beat the shit out of me and my girlfriend. She sensed that we needed to get together—all of us—and just look at each other, simply because some of us believe the hype. Though she may hope that the next step for most of us will involve joining her little Nation of Islam, the majority won't and they may go home with a renewed respect for one another and a greater commitment to social change. Some of us *can* separate Newton from the Law of Gravity.

Moreover, Miss Khan coordinated an all-male gathering that the Black Woman on the Street did not receive as sexist, regardless of what certain intellectuals had to say. I saw the Black Woman on the Street waiting for the U Street bus, up in Adams Morgan, and in the Amtrak station. She said, "I'm very proud of our black men. Y'all got it together." And then she smiled a 440-watt smile. (pp. 39–40)

This unusual presence of Gaylect in written form represents a doubly marginalized community—the march about which Hannaham (1995) writes manifests the marginalization of Black males, but then the Black Gay male is marginalized even further by the community to which he belongs. He must show his allegiance to the march by celebrating his participation in it; yet, furthermore, he parodies the symbolized leadership (Louis Farrakhan) to state his indignation at the leader's sexualized bigotry. His method of doing this is not to attack the importance of the march ("she managed to pull off a much-needed if only precursory step in the self-determination of black American men"), but to parody the symbol itself ("I slam and lick him" replacing "Salaam-As-Salaikum"). This author performs a linguistic makeover and turns Louis Farrakhan into Miss Louise-Farrah Khan; Miss Khan is then forced to compositionally join the ranks of that which he opposes. "Her" diatribes are translated into Gaylect, and deconstructed with the adversary's language. Gay images such as RuPaul's 4 minute 40 second version of "You Better Work" are used to demonstrate the absolute absurdity of Miss Khan's logic.

An obvious characteristic of Gaylect that surfaces in this essay is the pronominal gender shift. The standardized use of pronouns designating males and females is displaced by a new set of pronoun rules. Gay men reconstruct the language as a means to defy the linguistic hegemony, thus defying the social hegemony. Patriarchy and heterosexism join ranks, placing Gay men in the social stigma of another marginalized, oppressed group—women. Because women's speech and activities are devalued, and because Gay men choose to do what patriarchy perceives as taking the roles of women, "feminized" language and "feminine" signs (*she*) are diminished. As exemplified in the preceding article, Gay men reapply this linguistic tool to then parody patriarchy. This kind of pronominal shift has been read as an insult to women, and I'm sure that in some cases it serves the misogyny that exists in the Gay male world. I think, though, that it is crucial to recognize the penultimate hegemonic force (which often conquers and divides) and place our energies accordingly.

In returning to Hannaham's (1995) parodying of Farrakhan, what the author does is referred to as *shade* in the Gay vernacular, as explained by the late New York drag diva Dorian Cory (Livingston, 1990):

> Shade comes from reading. Reading came first. Reading is the real art form of insult. You get in a smart crack and everyone laughs, and kikis because you found a flaw and exaggerated it, then you've got a good read going. If it's happening between the gay world and the straight world it's not really a read, it's more of insult, a vicious slur fight. But it's how they develop a sense of how to read. They may call you a faggot or a drag queen, you'll find something to call them. But then when you are all of the same thing then you have to go the fine points. In other words, if I'm a black queen and you're a black queen then we can't call each other black queen. That's not a read, that's just a fact. Then we talk about your ridiculous shape, your saggy face, your tacky class. Then reading became a developed form where it became shade. Shade is I don't tell you you're ugly but I don't have to tell you because you know you're ugly and that's shade.

Dorian Cory defines *shade* from a perspective within the discourse community, one that could not be formulated within a Webster's dictionary because of its specialized context. This form of linguistic insult in Gaylect not only functions as a means to express events or feelings that cannot be expressed with "straight" speech, but it has also evolved into a means of protection. For a group that has been ridiculed, language acts as a venue to verbally protect oneself; it becomes, as Cory clarifies, a "developed" mode of expression that can be used inside or outside the Gay community. Gaylect has developed a security system, a way to verbally retaliate when attacked. When the homophobe accosts you with "Pansy" or "Faggot," or a vicious queen insults you with Gaylect, you may be "fierce with shade" (aptly prepared with the linguistic power to retort in that exchange).

Similar examples of written Gaylect are often evident in Michael Musto's column in the New York weekly newspaper the *Village Voice*. His use of parody, wordplay, and reference seem exemplary of what I would call rhetorically Gay. In a retort to Jerry Falwell's outing of Tinky Winky (the purple Teletubby with the triangular head-antenna), Musto (1999) sends a clearly Queer message that marks itself with its use of Gaylect:

> And typically, [Falwell debated against the children's character] without much backup, readily admitting that he's never even seen *Teletubbies*. (Funny, it's designed for this intellectual peer group—and it's the only show on PBS that is.) "I believe that role-modeling the gay lifestyle is damaging to the moral lives of children," Jerry told the press, clearly nervous that, years from now, all those

'Tubbies watchers will robotically choose anal penetration as a result of their babyhood viewing practices. Alas, Jerry's off on some of the details. In his esteemed *National Liberty Journal*, he wrote that Tinky's purple skin tone is the color of gay pride, "and his antenna is shaped like a triangle—the gay pride symbol." Pardon my rainbow, but I seem to remember that *lavender* is more of an out shade and a *pink* triangle is actually the symbol—though I may be betraying my own Martha Stewart-loving sisterhood here. It doesn't really matter anyway, since there are enough other queer signifiers to justify Falwell's gay panic. Tinky carries a patent-leather handbag, prances around in a tutu, and does pretty much all the same things I do. He's so gay, in fact, that he verges on a stereotype—he's as flaming as Richard Simmons, Bert, Ernie, and one of those kids on *Barney* combined. (Come on, *you* know which one.)

Musto constructs his argument not by directly attacking Falwell's "issues," but by presenting the Reverend's own statements as self-evident nonsense that need only casual debriefing. In fact, Musto begins his article with the statement, "Here's a first: I'm totally aligned with the Reverend Jerry Falwell! I thoroughly agree with the guy that Tinky Winky is a Pansy Wansy—we only seem to differ on what to *make* of this information." According to Musto, more idiotic than Falwell's logic is his inability to distinguish colors and other Queer fashion accessories correctly. I can hear Musto and his readers sucking their teeth at Falwell: "Pardon my rainbow,"[5] but any member of the Martha Stewart–loving sisterhood would know lavender from purple. The columnist continues by actually listing Tinky Winky's Queer attributes, fueling Falwell's diatribe. Musto's rhetorical strategy is not *straight*forwardly adversarial but, instead, undercuts the argument by showing just how clueless the Reverend is about Queer semiotics. If you're going to denounce Queer lifestyle, at least know what it is. Musto uses his tone, vocabulary, and sense of what his Queer-friendly audience will know to destroy Falwell's credibility. If I may use a topical metaphor to describe his argumentative strategy, Musto draws Falwell close with conciliatory agreement, only to coldcock him with his rhetorical handbag. With the information that Falwell provides, Musto *makes* a mocking, uncompromising *tour de force*: Tinky Winky is a Pansy Wansy—SO WHAT?

Musto's (1999) forthright rejoinder is a clear example of *shade*. It shares many of the rhetorical attributes that Hannaham (1995) used in his article on the Million Man March: playfulness, parody, and a reliance on the reader to "get it." The "getting it" depends on the readers' knowledge of Queer semiotics but, also, on their Queer linguistics—what some might call *camp*, what I call Gaylect. These writers are aware that their Queer-friendly audience has had enough experience with the "glass closet" to recognize the evident Gayness of a particular contingency of the Million Man March and of some of the cartoon characters that we habitually see but continue to overlook. How long have

---

[5]Get it?—rainbow, another Queer symbol.

Bert and Ernie lived together? As Musto comments in his article, "While Jerry's convinced that the Teletubby's supposed gayness is a menace to society, I feel it teaches kids the welcome lesson that it takes all types to make up the world, from purple, flouncy moppets to blue-in-the-face windbags."

These Queer writers, and others who use Gaylect, share a similar linguistic and rhetorical style that has a recognizable style and a distinguishable sensibility from conventional—what I will venture to call—"Straight" talk. "Straight" talk or heteronormative language patterns remain elusive like "Whiteness" does in racial studies. Because it has historically become the gauge on which all else is metered, it often remains a "silent partner" in the analytic transaction. Comparative rhetoric has come under similar criticism because it "privileged the writing of [the] native English speaker" (Connor, 1996, p. 16) as a monolithic form against which to compare all other rhetorical work. As I became more familiar with contrastive rhetoric, I was attracted by those theorists who looked at the writing of first-language learners. The social constructivists Berkenkotter and Huckin (1993) created a theoretical framework in which I was able to situate my own ideas about sociolinguistics. It was not surprising to me that I shared many of the theoretical influences they used to develop their framework—Bakhtin, Vygotsky, ethnographic methodologies. Many of my own ideas about teaching, learning, and language usage relied on similar speculative groundings. Berkenkotter and Huckin's framework presented the following five principles:

1. Dynamism: Genres are dynamic rhetorical forms that develop from responses to recurrent situations and serve to stabilize experience and give it coherence and meaning. Genres change over time in response to their user's sociocognitive needs.

2. Situatedness: Our knowledge of genres is derived from and embedded in our participation in the communicative activities of daily and professional life. As such, genre knowledge is a form of "situated cognition," which continues to develop as we participate in the activities of the culture.

3. Form and content: Genre knowledge embraces both form and content, including a sense of what content is appropriate to a particular situation at a particular point in time.

4. Duality of structure: As we draw on genre rules to engage in professional activities, we *constitute* social structures (in professional, institutional, and organizational contexts) and simultaneously *reproduce* these structures.

5. Community ownership: Genre conventions signal a discourse community's norms, epistemology, ideology, and social ontology. (p. 478)

These five principles strongly resonate with the research I have done on Gaylect. The social and linguistic dynamics of these urban Queer groups have created a shared language that "stabilizes experience" within the Gay community, giving it "coherence and meaning." Furthermore, its language progressively changes, dependent on its constituency's needs. Likewise, Gaylect has developed out of certain activities that have occurred within this community. The people who use it share a sense of when and how it is appropriate. It serves to create a solidarity within the community, while also responding to the forces that oppose it. Sometimes, in fact, Gay men need to "code-switch" out of Gaylect as a means of personal safety, job security, or familial stability in less than homophile environments. This feature of entering and exiting Gaylect signals Berkenkotter and Huckin's (1993) duality of structure, because the social conventions of Gaylect are simultaneously subsumed within the social conventions of a larger, dominant culture that some Queer theorists would call heterosexism or heteronormativity. The men who use Gaylect are aware of how, when, and why their specialized linguistic roles are positioned in society. Finally, Gaylect exhibits the norms, epistemology, ideology, and social ontology of the Gay male community of Manhattan, perhaps of other locales as well. This group expresses both its shared and conflicting ideas in specific ways idiosyncratic to that discourse community. Throughout this chapter, my examples and analyses illustrate how these five principles borrowed from contrastive rhetoric theory dialogue with my own ideas about Gaylect. I attempt to describe and place Gaylect, so that it may speak to the needs of its particular community, while also addressing its potential benefits to other communities, specifically learning communities. Members of the Queer community learn quickly how they may use language, where and how it may be used, and with whom. If they do not make these conscious/conscientious choices (which rely on a learned linguistic and self-awareness), they risk missing opportunities of intimacy within their own community and/or the safety that does not always exist outside their enclaves.

In the context of contrastive rhetoric, I reviewed my research and the references that inspired it and recognized that, in fact, looking at how language characteristics transferred and were used when members moved from one linguistic community to another was a major theme in my Gaylect study. My initial questions as I began this inquiry were: How can the language of Gay men correspond with contrastive rhetoric? How can the language of Gay men inform, or even relate to, contrastive rhetoric's investigations and the second-language learners it often studies? Furthermore, if certain comparative connections can be made to Gay language, how productive will they be in contrastive rhetoric's particular brand of language theory, and who may gain from it? Without addressing these issues, I felt that I would underestimate the potentials for contrastive rhetoric theory, while disregarding how linguistic studies in general can address social problems and improve people's lives.

The advantage of making explicit to all of society what is self-evidently Queer is that it begins to erode a society's self-deception. In *Epistemology of the Closet*, Eve Sedgwick (1990) wisely advised that the "open-secret structure" can be "unpredictably weird," sometimes damaging, and that not until we reveal the secret can we make change: "In dealing with an open-secret structure, it's only by being shameless about risking the obvious that we happen into the vicinity of the transformative" (p. 22). If things are to change for Gay men and Lesbians, maybe we should all invest in paying attention to the qualities of their language, not as a means to identify and ridicule their lispy sibilance or husky butchness but as a way to figure out how one community makes meaning in the world. This has been contrastive rhetoric's project from the beginning: to see how people's cultural differences affect their ability to express and, therefore, negotiate with and adapt to their linguistic and social surroundings. If done well, all similar sociolinguistic studies of marginalized groups create the sites at which discourses disintegrate long-held and unchallenged positions about the Other, about Difference. In careful and compassionate research about people's linguistic behaviors, real differences may be recorded, discussed, and reasoned into the various social and historical ingredients that make up our individual identities and, synchronously, our societies. Language inquiry is a place to start learning about Gays and Lesbians, people of other races, creeds, and classes, second-language students, underprepared students—all the people whose habits, linguistic and otherwise, perplex us. Dialogues based on observed facts about compared groups and cultures may then be the source of resolve, rather than the myths created by stereotyping and simplification.

REFERENCES

Austin, H. M. (1988). *Gay(s) language: A dic(k)tionary of gay slang.* Austin, TX: Bannea Books.

Bakhtin, M. M. (1981). *The dialogic imagination* (M. Holquist, Ed.). Austin: University of Texas Press.

Berkenkotter, C., & Huckin, T. N. (1993, October). Rethinking genre from a sociocognitive perspective. *Written Communication, 10,* 475–509.

Butler, J. P. (1990). *Gender trouble: Feminism and the subversion of identity.* New York: Routledge.

Butler, J. P. (1997). *Excitable speech: A politics of the performative.* New York: Routledge.

Chesebro, J. W. (1981). *Gayspeak: Gay male and lesbian communication.* New York: Pilgrim Press.

Connor, U. (1996). *Contrastive rhetoric.* New York: Cambridge University Press.

Gaudio, R. P. (1997). Not talking straight in Hausa. In A. Livia & K. Hall (Eds.), *Queerly phrased: Language, gender, and sexuality* (pp. 430–460). New York: Oxford University Press.

Groff, D. (1990, June). Taking the test. *Wigwag,* 47–49.

Hall, K. (1997). "Go suck your husband's sugarcane!": Hijras and the use of sexual insult. In A. Livia & K. Hall (Eds.), *Queerly phrased: Language, gender, and sexuality* (pp. 402–415). New York: Oxford University Press.

Hannaham, J. (1995, October 31). Nothin' but a g-string. *Village Voice,* 39–40.

Leap, W. L. (1996). *Word's out: Gay men's English.* Minneapolis: University of Minnesota Press.

Levin, J. (1983). *Reflections on the American homosexual rights movement.* New York: Gai Saber Monograph.

Livia, A. (1997). Disloyal to masculinity: Linguistic gender and liminal identity in French. In A. Livia & K. Hall (Eds.), *Queerly phrased: Language, gender, and sexuality* (pp. 349–368). New York: Oxford University Press.

Livia, A., & Hall, K. (Eds.). (1997). *Queerly phrased: Language, gender, and sexuality.* New York: Oxford University Press.

Livingston, J. (Director/Producer), Finch, N., & Lacy, D. (Executive Producers). (1990). *Paris is burning* [Film]. New York: Insight Media.

Manalansan, M. F., IV. (1995). "Performing" the Filipino gay experiences in America: Linguistic strategies in a transnational context. In W. L. Leap (Ed.), *Beyond the lavender lexicon* (pp. 249–266). Amsterdam: Gordon & Breach.

Meyer, M. (Ed.). (1994). *The politics and poetics of camp.* New York: Routledge.

Musto, M. (1999, February 17–23). Purple passion. *Village Voice* [On-line]. Available: Netscape: www.villagevoice.com

Ogawa, N., & Smith, J. S. (1997). The gendering of the gay male sex class in Japan: A case study based on *Rasen No Sobyò.* In A. Livia & K. Hall (Eds.), *Queerly phrased: Language, gender, and sexuality* (pp. 402–415). New York: Oxford University Press.

Pastre, G. (1997). Linguistic gender play among French gays and lesbians. In A. Livia & K. Hall (Eds.), *Queerly phrased: Language, gender, and sexuality* (pp. 369–379). New York: Oxford University Press.

Purves, A. C. (Ed.). (1988). *Writing across languages and cultures: Issues in contrastive rhetoric.* Newbury Park, CA: Sage.

Sedgwick, E. K. (1990). *Epistemology of the closet.* Berkeley: University of California Press.

Sontag, S. (1966). *Against interpretation and other essays.* New York: Farrar, Straus & Giroux.

Springer, R. J. (Ed.). (1994). *Queer words, queer images: Communication and the construction of homosexuality.* New York: New York University Press.

Afterword

Why Revisit/Redefine Contrastive Rhetoric Theory?

Fred Reynolds
City College of the City University of New York

Contrastive Rhetoric Revisited and Redefined has done a number of important things that deserve some kind of closing comment, and so I am honored that my good friend and former student Clayann Gilliam Panetta invited me to contribute to her first book by offering a short summary of why I think it matters, and why I encouraged her and her publisher, Lawrence Erlbaum Associates (LEA), to do it in the first place. As we enter the new millenium, Rhetoric and Composition Studies certainly suffers from no shortage of edited essay collections on topics of interest to its students, scholars, and observers, and so an obvious question is why in the world we need another one. To my thinking, there are at least four answers to that question.

First, we need it because of its main point. In its very eclecticism and expansiveness, *Contrastive Rhetoric Revisited and Redefined* makes the important and useful argument that contrastive rhetoric theory (CRT) can and should be used as an umbrella under which we might assemble a much wider range of "difference rhetoric" discussions and analyses than Kaplan, Connor, Leki, and other CRT pioneers may have originally envisioned. In the sense that it asks us to consider how broad and rich and central the study of rhetorical differences beyond the surface level can be—that it says, "Look at the sheer range of things we might examine under the masthead of CRT"—this volume extends, expands, applies, and provokes and, in so doing, represents the very best traditions of Rhetoric and Composition scholarship.

Second, we need it because of its collection of sources, references, and citations. *Contrastive Rhetoric Revisited and Redefined* brings together in a single volume a wealth of references and footnote trails that students and scholars will be able to use as the springboard for the next generation of work on what Robert

Kaplan has rightly referred to in this volume as the "complex, multifaceted, multidimensional set" of language issues for which he coined the very term "contrastive rhetoric" more than three decades ago. Consider, just to cite one example, the fourth footnote in Kaplan's Foreword to this volume, the footnote in which he assembles for us a stunning list of studies that have been done on more "second" languages than most of us probably knew existed. And if Kaplan, Connor, and Leki ever doubted that their work had mattered, they might reflect on the sheer number of times that they are cited by this volume's contributors.

Third, we need it because several of its individual chapters can have a profound effect on what we teach and how we teach it. At the risk of being accused of playing favorites—let me just confess that I have long been and continue to be a fan of this woman's work—I think Kristin Woolever's chapter in this volume (chap. 4), the one on rhetorical contrasts in the business and technical professions, is the most useful analysis of issues and strategies in international communication that I have seen to date. Similarly, Mark McBeth's chapter on "the queen's English" (chap. 8) strikes me as especially rich; it's amusing, daring, provocative, and, above all, very pedagogically useful. Like Woolever's contribution to the volume, it challenges the notion that current work in Rhetoric and Composition tends to suffer from the theoretical vapors, that it plays a glass bead game with little practical significance.

Fourth, we need this book because, in it, Kaplan and Connor speak. In *Contrastive Rhetoric Revisited and Redefined* we get to hear precisely what two of CRT's pioneers actually think about what younger scholars have done and are still doing with their work, and I think this is a real treat. It pained me, for example, when I assembled my 1995 LEA essay collection on some of the revisitations and redefinitions of classical memory and delivery as something bigger and better than memorizing and gesticulating speeches, that I never got to hear how Corbett and other pioneers in classical rhetoric felt about what my contributors and I were suggesting and arguing for in our work. If such things matter, and I think they do, then here we get a glimpse of what some of our heroes think about some of our appropriations.

Finally, I would close by noting that, with the publication of this volume, Lawrence Erlbaum Associates has once again provided a quality home for the production and support of a good new research project in Rhetoric and Composition Studies at a time when many academic book publishers increasingly take risks on nothing other than sure-sells. That, to me, is one final reason why *Contrastive Rhetoric Revisited and Redefined* matters.

Panetta, her colleagues, and LEA have given us something of value in this volume. By revisiting/redefining contrastive rhetoric theory, they have confirmed our enterprise and suggested new lenses through which we might look to the future.

About the Contributors

Anne Bliss is a senior instructor and the coordinator for English as a Second Language (ESL) in the university writing program at the University of Colorado, Boulder, where she currently teaches both traditional and Web-based writing courses. Her research interests in comparative and contrastive rhetoric complement her research in language acquisition, rhetorical structures, and the interplay of computers and other technologies with rhetoric and writing. She has also worked as a teacher trainer and student instructor in Russia, Vietnam, and China. Off campus, she is well known for her work with handcrafted textiles and natural dyes, and she has taught and published extensively in this area. She holds a master's degree in linguistics, and her doctoral research in education evaluated an intensive training program for international students entering American and Canadian universities.

Juanita Comfort is an assistant professor of English at Old Dominion University, Norfolk, Virginia, where she teaches first-year and advanced composition, technical writing, and graduate courses in rhetoric. She has presented papers at the Conference on College Composition and Communication, Rhetoric Society of America, and Penn State Conference on Rhetoric and Composition. Her article on college writers and Black feminist essays appears in the June 2000 issue of CCC. Currently, she is completing a book on personal disclosure, ethos, and self-identity in essays by Black feminist writers.

Ulla Connor is a professor of English at Indiana University at Indianapolis, where she directs the ESL program and ESL teacher training program. She has published widely on second-language reading and writing. She is coeditor of *Writing Across Languages: Analysis of L2 Test* and *Coherence in Writing: Research and Pedagogical Perspectives*. Most recently, she is the author of *Contrastive Rhetoric: Cross-Cultural Aspects of Second-Language Writing*.

Jan Corbett is assistant professor of English at Delaware Valley College, Doylestown, Pennsylvania, where she teaches composition and communication. She has published in the *Technical Communication Quarterly*, the *Journal of the Association for the Interdisciplinary Study of the Arts*, and the *Performing Arts Journal*. She holds the MS in communications and PhD in English from Temple University.

Robert B. Kaplan is Professor Emeritus of applied linguistics and past director of the American Language Institute, University of Southern California, where he was a member of the faculty since 1960, retiring on January 1, 1995. In 1998–1999, he served as professor of applied linguistics in the Graduate School of Applied Language Study, Meikai University, Japan. Dr. Kaplan is the past editor-in-chief and currently a member of the editorial board of the *Annual Review of Applied Linguistics*, which he founded in 1980; he is also editor-in-chief of the *Handbook of Applied Linguistics* and a member of the editorial board of the Oxford University Press *International Encyclopedia of Linguistics*, and he serves on the editorial boards of several scholarly journals. He has authored or edited 35 books, more than 135 articles in scholarly journals and chapters in books, and more than 85 book reviews and other ephemeral pieces in various newsletters, as well as 9 special reports to government in the United States and elsewhere. Over a relatively long career, he has presented more than 200 talks, papers, and invited plenary addresses at national and international conferences. He has specialized in written discourse analysis, and his name has been widely linked with the notion of contrastive rhetoric.

Mark McBeth has been working in the field of English composition at the City College of New York for the past 6 years. During that time, he has administered a writing program, designed special curricula and courses, counseled students, facilitated teaching seminars, and directed a writing center. He is finishing his PhD research at the Graduate Center of the City University of New York. In his dissertation, he investigates how composition and Queer theories converge to inform questions of desire and education, which, subsequently, lead to students' learning pleasures.

Laura Micciche is assistant professor of English at East Carolina University, where she teaches courses in writing, rhetorical theory, composition studies, and feminist rhetorics. Her reviews and articles have appeared in *Composition Studies/Freshman English News*, *Composition Forum*, and *American Studies International*.

Clayann Gilliam Panetta is a visiting assistant professor of English at Christian Brothers University in Memphis, Tennessee, where she teaches various writing courses. Previously, she was the writing center director at Mercyhurst College in Erie, Pennsylvania, where she has created and conducted training programs for writing consultants, acted as a liaison between the writing program and faculty in other disciplines, and taught a variety of writing courses. Her publications and presentations reflect a research agenda that focuses primarily on cross-cultural issues in writing, classical rhetoric's application to modern rhetoric, and computer-assisted composition. She holds a BA in English from Blue Mountain College (Blue Mountain, MS) and an MA and PhD from Old Dominion University (Norfolk, VA) in composition studies.

Fred Reynolds is professor of English and director of the graduate program in language and literacy at the City College of the City University of New York. He is the author/editor of *Rhetorical Memory and Delivery: Classical Concepts for Contemporary Composition and Communication* (1993, Lawrence Erlbaum Associates), *Professional Writing in Context: Lessons From Teaching and Consulting in Worlds of Work* (1995, Lawrence Erlbaum Associates), and *Rhetoric, Cultural Studies, and Literacy: Selected Papers From the 1994 Conference of the Rhetoric Society of America* (1995, Lawrence Erlbaum Associates), and with David Mair and Pamela Fischer, *Writing and Reading Mental Health Records: Issues and Analysis in Professional Writing and Scientific Rhetoric* (1995, Lawrence Erlbaum Associates). He received BA, MA, and MA degrees in speech communication and English from Midwestern State University, and a PhD in composition studies from the University of Oklahoma.

Dené Scoggins is an assistant professor of English at Texas Wesleyan University. Her research interests include ESL issues, computer technologies for the classroom, Renaissance literature, history of science, and postmodern theory. She has presented papers at several national and international conferences in the fields of composition and literature. She is currently working on a book project dealing with history of science issues in Renaissance texts. She received her doctorate from the University of Texas at Austin, where she wrote her dissertation on astrology in Dante, Rabelais, Shakespeare, and Milton.

Kristen R. Woolever is a professor of English at Northeastern University in Boston, where she directs the graduate programs in technical and professional writing and the writing program in the School of Law. She has published widely on rhetoric, technical communication, and legal writing, and she consults with business and industry nationally and internationally.

Author Index

129

Subject Index